TAT
THAT IS BRAHMAN

A 21ˢᵗ Century Bhagavad Gita summary

Realising Ishvara - Brahman

Decoded into byte sized wisdom *sutras*.

Volume 2
Chapters 7 -12

ANURADHA MAHAJAN
DR. SAJNI VAIDYA

INDIA · SINGAPORE · MALAYSIA

ISBN
Hardcase 979-8-89724-940-4
Paperback 979-8-89673-366-9

Tat as *Brahman*

Ishvara: Brahman in Creation

Who is Brahman? What is Brahman? Why is Brahman?

The Omniscient - the Omnipresent - the Omnipotent

Dedication

TAT is dedicated to the guru-preceptors, the masters of humanity. Tat is a very special celebration, an offering of love, regards, gratitude, honor, and homage to the lineage of masters from whom we learn, starting with the ultimate source – Ishvara and continuing to the present-day Gurus and Sages.

We dedicate the content to Sri Sri Parmahansa Yogananda, whose life and teachings have inspired humanity.

Parmahansa means 'The Supreme Swan' (which has the power of distilling pure milk from a mixture of milk and water) and is recognized as the symbol of spiritual discrimination (Vivek).

This is a title of honor given to a sage who has become enlightened and is equally comfortable, in the realms of both matter and spirit.

We dedicate this body of work to the learned and realized Gurus who have generously shared this knowledge with humanity.

The English transliteration of the Sanskrit verses of the Bhagavad Gita have been taken from Sri Sri Parmahansa Yogananda's 'Royal Science of God Realisation – God Talks with Arjuna'

"From Joy I came, for Joy I live,

in sacred Joy I melt.

Ocean of mind, I drink all Creation's waves,

Four veils of solid, liquid, vapour, light,

Lift aright

I, in everything, enters the great Myself,

Eternity and I, One united ray

A tiny bubble of laughter, I

Am become the sea of Mirth itself"

Sri Sri Parmahansa Yogananda

Contents

<u>Foreword</u>

The Bhagavad Gita is a timeless treasure of wisdom from ancient India, that was given by Sri Krishna to Arjuna at the start of the epoch that ended with the Mahabharata war.

Krishna's teachings seem to resound in every generation, as he shows Arjuna a path to fulfil his duty selflessly and without care for reward, as well as to live life as a *yajña*, a sacred offering, dedicated to a higher purpose.

This allowed Arjuna to be in the midst of action in spite of the chaos all around, yet be inwardly still and silent, always in the present, and ever focused on his purpose.

When we can live life as a *yajña*, where we give more than we take from this world, with a heart full of compassion and unconditional loving kindness, with a firm will and determination and in a spirit of service, then we would have lived a fulfilled life. The message of the Gita has been refreshed over the millennia, for each generation by sages, writers and earnest seekers.

In fact, it was said that if you wished to start a new school of *Vedānta* philosophy, you had to write a unique commentary on the Gita, Upanishads and Brahma Sutra.

We are fortunate that Anuradha Mahajan and Dr. Sajni Vaidya's sacred offering is this work **TAT**, which aims to bring the ancient teachings of Krishna to the modern seeker. Anu and Sajni have dedicated this study, in a quest to share their understanding of the ancient wisdom of India, to many around the world.

We hope that this 2nd Volume of **TAT** (preceded by **TVAM** - Volume 1) inspires the reader to bring the messages of the Gita into their everyday life and spiritual practice.

There is no better act of service that Anu and Sajni could have done for us, and we are extremely grateful for their efforts.

Enjoy the sincere study of **TAT** and make the Gita live through you!

Subhanu Saxena,

Chairman, Bharatiya Vidya Bhavan, London, UK

The Bhagavad Gita as our Guide through Life

18 Chapters – 700 Verses

Chapters 1– 6 deal with **TVAM** (Individual Soul / Atman) and predominantly focus on Karma and Samkhya Yoga. (Volume 1)

Amazon link:

https://www.amazon.in/TVAM-21st-Century-Bhagavad-Summary/dp/B0CZ9FML53

Notion Press link:

https://notionpress.com/read/tvam

Chapters 7–12 deal with **TAT** (Supreme Consciousness - Brahman) and predominantly focus on Bhakti Yoga. (Volume 2)

Upcoming Publication:

Chapters 13–18 deal with **ASI** or essence of the knowledge in the Bhagavad Gita and can be summarized in the Mahavakya 'Tat Tvam Asi' – 'That Thou Art.' (Volume 3)

Asi is when the Knowledge, the Knower and the Known all become One. **Asi** is the connection between **Tvam** and **Tat.**

In this Volume 3, the manner and the techniques of how TVAM can merge with TAT are described.

To the reader:

When reading the text of this Gita study, we ask the readers to be aware of the following format:

1. Verses spoken by Sri Krishna in **bold**

2. Verses spoken by Arjuna in normal typeface

3. Sanskrit words in Italic typeface

4. A simple translation of the verses from Sanskrit to English using Sri Paramhansa Yogananda's books God Talks with Arjuna and Royal Science of God Realisation

5. Explanations and esoteric interpretations of the verses by the authors are inspired by Sri Paramhansa Yogananda's teachings.

6. Clarifications and meanings provided through the medium of flow charts, illustrations and tables are created by the authors, unless mentioned otherwise.

7. Tasks are a tool, to be completed by the reader to enhance their own understanding.

8. Brahman is also referred to as the Supreme Source, Supreme Consciousness, the Absolute Truth, Sat, Lord, He, Him, God & Godhead.

9. When 'self' reflects ego 's' is small and when Self is used for Atman or Soul 'S' is in Capital.

Disclaimer: The flowcharts presented in this volume are only an indication of the processes explained in the text, which may be helpful as an aid to our study. However, these are limited and constrained in their projections and hence should not be considered as exact depictions.

<u>Introduction by the Authors</u>

We attempt here to pen down the essence of the Srimad Bhagavad Gita in simple words as it unfolded during our twelve-year study, a journey of research and insight into the true purpose of our life and the ways to achieve our full potential. TAT is the second part of a three-part series.

We hope this book will be a guide to everyone who has one or more questions, is curious, wants to learn about the mysteries of life and is also caught up between doubts, ignorance and convictions that are difficult to shake off.

Gita is a bridge between what we are and what we want to be; where we are and where we wish to be. The basic concepts are well established, and perceptions may differ from person to person, but the essence needs to be absorbed and incorporated in our daily routines with whatever small things we can do. Small steps lead to a bigger change leading to change in our mindsets which makes us more in control of our actions and reactions in our daily routine.

We aspire to inspire the reader with the message that Self-realisation is not an unachievable goal but possible through leading a disciplined life along with spiritual practices of meditation and scriptural studies. The Human being has immense unutilized, unrecognized potential. The Geeta shows us how to tap that potential and live a more fulfilled life free of miseries.

The intent of this text is for us to understand and experience our true identity as *Aham Brahmasmi*– I am that Supreme Self.

Reading **Tat** may hopefully awaken within us a connection with Divinity that we may already be aware of, yet to fully know but that which we are silently seeking. The magical alignment of all three – knowledge, knowing and the known – is what the Bhagavad Gita leads us to.

Gita is not something we can absorb in one time; every time we read it, we find a new dimension, as it varies with how we perceive it and in which frame of mind we are reading it.

Our ultimate goal: experiencing universal love, peace, joy, bliss of the soul and freedom from miseries, eventually leading us to Self-realisation and 'Divine Union' (Yuj).

We would like to apologize if any of our understanding that is inked in this version is perceived as erroneous or misrepresented. Our pure intent is to bring forth this incredible esoteric knowledge to the reader.

The Bhagavad Gita is not only Vedanta but also a Moksha Shastra. (a scripture leading us to liberation). It explains beautifully, how this Mahavakya **Tat Tvam Asi** is possible. **Tat** is Brahman, **Tvam** is the individual Self and **Asi** is the merging of Tvam with Tat.

The Bhagavad Gita means an eternal divine song. Why would the good Lord want to talk of this beautiful philosophy in the battlefield? Because bringing music and wisdom to the battlefield, indicates an eternal divine phenomenon.

The universe is made of conflict and battle between uplifting forces and delusive forces - It is unavoidable. Harmony can be brought only by wisdom and divinity. Conflict is there not only in the universe, but in each one of us as well.

We commence with a short scene from the great epic, Mahabharata. The Mahabharata is an allegory of our daily psychological and spiritual battle within the human body.

After all, our world, our life is also a Kurukshetra, a field of action. Here we perform daily actions with our body which has physical, mental and soul faculties. It is also a Dharmakshetra, a field of righteous action. we are making daily choices in our mind, choosing many a times between what is right and what is wrong. Our life is a constant battle between life and death, knowledge and ignorance, health and sickness, self-control and giving in to temptation, changing and changelessness guided by our intelligence and moral values.

The conflict depicted in this superb tome is between the pure discriminative intellect *(buddhi)*, which is in tune with the vibration of the super soul **vs.** the blind, sense infatuated mind *(manas)*, which is under the delusive influence of the ego *(aham)* that has lost the memory of its precursor.

Why the Mahabharata? The 100,000-verse tome contains in its midst a 700-verse jewel – the Bhagavad Gita; the immortal dialogue between Arjuna and Sri Krishna on a battlefield, Kurukshetra (symbolic of our bodily field).

The much-venerated Sage Ved Vyas has been credited as the compiler of the Vēdās (as it is) into four classifications. He is the author of the 18 Puranas, the Brahma sutras and the Mahabharata and compiled the Bhagavad Gita, which is encapsulated deep within the Mahabharata. Much like the texts of other religions, the Bhagavad Gita was revealed by the Supreme Lord, intuited directly by the meditating Seer Ved Vyas, who is spoken of as a partial avatar and reincarnation of Lord Vishnu.

Sage Ved Vyasa received the Bhagavad Gita as a revelation and recorded it as a discourse. Ved Vyasa was a Rishi (a sage), who was continuously in divine union. He had the power to receive this knowledge from the ultimate source of divinity through his energized faculty of divine intuition.

Legend has it that Sage Ved Vyas asked the divine celestial Ganesh to pen down his large manuscript of 100,000 verses, while he recited them. Ganapati was the powerful Deva competent enough for this task. Ganesh acquiesced on the condition that he would write only in one continuous sitting, with no breaks.

After some thought, as Vyas had a gargantuan script to relay, he put forth his own condition. He agreed, provided that Ganesh would comprehend the verses before inking it.

Ved Vyas thus cleverly managed to get much-needed moments of respite when Ganpati would pause to introspect and reflect.

<u>Glossary 1 - A Brief Glossary of Terms</u>

- **BRAHMAN** – The Supreme Consciousness, the Ultimate Divine Source.

- **AHAM BRAHMASMI** - I am That (Brahman)

- **ABHASA CHAITANYA:** Reflected Spirit. (Reflection from universal spirit, also called Kutastha Chaitanya, on all material objects, by which they are spiritualized and energized).

- The **ABSOLUTE:** The One, The Creator, Supreme Being, Cosmic Consciousness, Spirit Beyond Creation, Essence of manifestation, Brahman

- **AHAMKARA OR DIVINE EGO OR UNIVERSAL EGO:** The first transformation, the sense of I as the experiencer. It is the pure ego of the causal body which individualizes the soul from the Supreme Spirit. The root cause of self-awareness

- **AKASHIC RECORDS:** Super ether of omniscience in which all events and all wisdom are permanently recorded

- **ATMAN** - The Self

- **AVIDYA:** Ignorance or Delusion

- **BUDDHI:** Discriminating **Intellect**. It is one of the four aspects of *antahakaran.* Positive aspect of the mind. The intellectual faculty to discern, judge, comprehend, understand something.

- **CHAITANYA:** Pure Consciousness, Awareness.

- **MAHA PRAKRITI**: Holy Ghost, Creative Mother Nature that, through cosmic vibration of its own self, brings into manifestation all creation.

- **CHITTA:** Intuitive feeling. It is one of the four aspects of the *antahakaran.* It is also the storehouse of memory of all past and present lives. The intelligent consciousness, the power of feeling and the basic mental consciousness.

- **CHAKRAS:** Energy centres in the astral spine. Each chakra is associated with a quality of consciousness, an element & a planet.

The seven chakras in order of location in the spine:

Mooladhara chakra: at the base of the spine, coccygeal centre, vibratory earth element, power of resistance

Svadhisthana chakra: an inch above the first chakra, sacral, vibratory water element, divine power of adherence

Manipura chakra: behind the navel, lumbar, vibratory fire element, Divine self-control

Anahata chakra: at the heart area, dorsal, vibratory ether element, divine calmness

Vishuddhi chakra: throat centre, cervical, vibratory air element, righteousness/dharma

Ajna (Agya) chakra: point between the eyebrows, third eye-centre for wisdom.

Sahasrara chakra: crown chakra, at the top of the head, centre for Moksha.

- **ESOTERIC:** Deep, Secretive and Spiritual

- **EXOTERIC:** Material and Outward

- **HIRANYAGARBHA:** Is the eternal seed of the Macrocosm. The blueprint of the Universe, the governing deity of the Causal world of the Macrocosm.

- **INFINITE SPIRIT: Para Brahman**, God the father of creation: Transcendental unchanging source. It is present in every atom of creation.

- **ISHVARA:** Supreme Consciousness – Brahman in Creation

- **JNANA:** Ultimate Spiritual Knowledge resulting in realisation

- **JNANA AVATAR:** Incarnation of wisdom (Jnana is also Gyana)

- **KRIYA YOGA:** A sacred spiritual science, originating millenniums ago in India. It includes certain techniques of meditation, whose devoted practice leads to realisation of God

- **KUNDALINI:** Life force in the body centralized in the spine. The powerful current of creative life energy residing in a subtle coiled passageway at the base of the spine.

- **KUTASTHA CHAITANYA:** Universal unchangeable Spirit. Sanskrit word for kutastha is unchanged. Chaitanya is consciousness. God in creation

- **MACROCOSM:** The entire manifested universe. The whole, everything that exists.

- **MAHAT TATTVA:** The universal Intelligence. It refers to the great, primordial principle of the nature of both Spirit and matter, giving rise to the universal ego - As per Sankhya

Yog, it is the first evolute of prakriti. The causeless cause of the world, that is generated after prakriti begins to evolve when its equilibrium is disturbed, which causes expansion of material energy and matter.

- **MANAS:** The perceiving mind operating through the senses.

- **MATTER:** Earth, water, fire, air, ether.

- **MAYA:** The Magical measurer that makes the One appear as many, embracing their own individuality, forms and intelligences, existing in apparent separation from their Creator

- **MEDULLA OBLONGATA:** This structure at the base of the brain (top of the spinal cord) is the principal point of entry of life force (prana) into the body. The subtle centre at the medulla is the main switch that controls the entrance, storage and distribution of the life force.

- **MICROCOSM:** Man, or Mankind - the part of the whole, representee in miniature of the Macrocosm, the Universe

- **MOKSHA:** Liberation from the cycle of karma and rebirth

- **PRANA:** Life force. It is a universal sea of energy that infuses and vitalizes all matter. This energy coalesces into subatomic particles and atoms which become the basic building blocks of all matter manifesting the physical world. It is the power that flows into all living forms and performs vital functions. It possesses an inherent intelligence enabling it to carry out life sustaining processes.

- **PURANAS:** Sacred books illustrating Vedic knowledge through historical and legendary tales of ancient India's avatars, saints and sages, kings and heroes

- **SAMADHI:** Is that state when the meditator and the object of meditation (GOD) become ONE. Where the cosmic dream delusion terminates and the ecstatic dream being awakens in oneness with the pure consciousness of the Supreme Being.... ever existing, ever conscious, ever new bliss.

- **SANATANA DHARMA: The** Eternal Universal Religion for Mankind

- **SANAYASA:** Complete renunciation. A Sanyasi is a renouncer of that egoity (ahamkara) which is ingrained as delusion within the self of man.

- **SAT CHIT ANANDA** - Truth Consciousness Bliss

- **SOUL:** Individualized spirit. Nature of soul is ever existing, ever conscious and joy

- **TATTVAS:** The essence of vibratory elements. They are parts or aspects of nature. Their presence or absence, permutation and combination play an important role in the creation of the diversity of worlds, their objects and beings; they are the building blocks of the whole material manifestation.

- **YOGA:** The timeless science of God Union

- **YOGAVATAR:** Incarnation of a perfect Yogi - Krishna or the Adi Yogi (Shiva)

- **YUGA:** Earthly periods of time cycles

Find the detailed complete Glossary 3 at the end of the book

This is the first ammended version of March 2025

Tool for spiritual studies and growth:

Jnana Yoga or path of wisdom can sometimes be spent analyzing scriptural textbooks. But the *Vedantic* way of spiritual realisation is through *Shravan* (listening to the *Shruti*), *Mannan* (perceiving through purified *buddhi*) and *Nidhidhyasanam* (becoming one with the scriptural truth).

The Vedantic method of gaining profound understanding where one goes within, can be implemented by:

Shravan (Listening)	*Mannan* (Reflection, Contemplation and *Chintan*)	*Nidhidhyasanam* (Assimilation, Introspection and Meditation)
We may not be fully processing the information that we are gathering.	This removes the obstacles in the mind such as doubts and confusions.	Then the Realisation dawns that this knowledge is real and is in harmony with existence. This is when synchronicity with thoughts and manifestation is prevalent.
At this stage we may have doubts as we are only hearing and listening.	*Chintan* / Contemplation dwelling, debating, assimilating, collecting, ruminating on the topic.	Putting the knowledge learnt into practice and making it part of our lives.
Simple listening, hearing with the mind, the ears, and the brain. Simply gaining Information.	Comprehensive understanding of the knowledge with clarity and becoming convinced of the same.	Living the knowledge after being convinced of the same.

Chart 1

The Maha Battle

Ten gruesome days after the Maha Battle had commenced, in the Kuru palace, four miles away from Kurukshetra, a new scene was unfolding...

Scene One - at the Palace

The Kauravas's blind ruler, King Dhritrashtra, is able to muster enough courage to ask Sanjaya to relate the events of the Maha Battle, only on the 10th day of its commencement.

Dhritrashtra says" What is happening on the battlefield, please tell me Sanjaya, I am getting very nervous"!

Sanjaya, known as the epitome of impartial interiorization, was blessed with telepathic vision granted to him by Ved Vyas.

Sanjaya, is empowered by a boon that grants him vision beyond the realms of time and space. He is able to clearly describe the events that unfolded on the battlefield, commencing from day one of the Mahabattle at Kurukshetra.

He starts to relay a seemingly live commentary, to the blind King Dhritrashtra, relating all the events from the very onset of the battle.

Esoteric understanding: This is how introspection works...With grace and surrender if one tunes into the Self within, with impartial interiorization, divine download of knowledge begins!

Sanjay starts by eliciting the conflict and grief that Arjuna is feeling even before the war commences.

He relates how Krishna had to use all his powers of persuasion to convince Arjuna to pick up his bow and arrow and aim it at the opposing forces of the Kaurava army.

Scene Two - at the Battlefield

"I will not fight!' Arjuna says as he lays down his bow at Krishna's feet. Krishna is perplexed.

"A bit too late for this regret, isn't it?" Krishna says aghast.

He commences a dialogue with Arjuna trying his very best to convince Arjuna that he must fight this "battle for Science of Righteous living or battle for **Dharma**"

Krishna - "You are not evil if you shed blood in this battle",

Arjuna - "Krishna, you are very cleverly not fighting. You have decided not to pick up arms during this battle. You will not accrue any sin! And I thought it was you who said that it is very wrong to kill".

Krishna - "If the war is to be fought for the victory of one's principles, right against wrong, then it is not evil".

"But who is to decide what is good and what is evil?"

The back-and-forth argument went on and on. It took Krishna all his encouraging, motivational, educational, tutoring skills to convince Arjuna to pick up his bow again.

Scene Three - back in the Palace

In the meanwhile, at the palace – Sanjay continues to give Dhritrashtra a day-by-day account of the ten days that have passed since the death of the first Kuru prince.

Dhritrashtra is consumed with sorrow and dismay at all the mindless violence that has carried on despite efforts by the elders to call a ceasefire. Devas, Avatars, Sages and mortal men were all together engaged in such a gruesome display of violence. Why is this? What is the reason for this **Mahabattle**?

Each combatant had some kind of superpower. Today we see these similar superpowers in Olympian sportspersons. The magic comes from their super mental strength that courses through the body and makes it perform apparently miraculous feats, which are otherwise impossible. Belief in oneself produces vibrations that metamorphize into inconceivable feats.

There was much pomp and ceremony attached to the armies, the King and all the personnel involved with the call to war.

It was almost approaching dusk by the time the battle could begin on day one. The impatient armies fell upon each other consumed by rage and ferocity, especially annoyed as they had been kept waiting for all these hours wearing full regalia, heavy armor and were tiring rapidly.

It lasted eighteen days before the battle had ended with only ten soldiers left standing!

Hastinapur had lost over a million and seven hundred fifty thousand men in this gruesome war.

Task 1: How many chapters and verses are in the Bhagavad Gita? How many verses are there in the Mahabharata?

Introduction to **Tat** - Bhakti Yoga

In Volume One - **Tvam**, the first six chapters of the Bhagavad-Gita based on *Samkhya Yoga and Karma Yoga*, are explained to the seekers of *Jnana* [the ultimate Knowledge].

Emerging from material existence, the seeker establishes that the highest and most profound goal for the human being or universal man is to attain communion with the Supreme Source. This realisation or Union is achieved by the embodied *atman* or soul through different processes of *yoga,* which is the Science of daily living to help bring out the best in us and achieve this Union.

In the first six chapters the understanding of **Tvam** was researched. These next six chapters unfold the knowledge of **Tat** or **Ishvara**, who is the Supreme Consciousness in creation - Kutastha Chaitanya. Kutastha means unchanging and Chaitanya is Consciousness.

The 'Me' that Lord Krishna refers himself as, throughout the verses is Him speaking as '**Ishvara**'.

It is to be noted that chapters 7-12 describe and elaborate on Brahman and how to unite with His vibration and merge unto Him aligning the self with the Supreme Self. These are known as the Chapters on *Bhakti Yoga.*

These six chapters, commonly known as the *Bhakti Yoga* section, elaborate on the science of the individual consciousness attaining communion with the ultimate Consciousness through loving devotion to the Supreme source. The subject matter revealed here is the nature of the Supreme Consciousness and the various modes of devotion and meditation that are to be offered to attain Him. The lessons in these chapters are magical and special.

We begin to realize that the divine source is within us. When we reflect on the Creators' projection and align with this divine vibration, we achieve clarity and the light of knowledge dawns within.

The more we learn about ourselves, the more we believe in ourselves, the more we grow and the more powerful and complete we become. Self-Realisation is indeed realisation of one's own powerful potential and the possibility of becoming one with the universe. Without this realisation, we hardly use a miniscule of the potential we are born with and capable of!

As per Vēdānta, the universe is Brahman's cosmic dream manifestation, and the seeker wants to know how to traverse this cosmos.

Surrender to the universe and the laws of creation are the key. Finding oneself in alignment to this higher frequency of vibration is true Bhakti. The ego has to become one with divinity. Losing the small self to merge with the Supreme Self is also Bhakti.

O Divine mother, she who showers elixir of Advaita on us, O mother of 18 chapters, I meditate on thee, O Srimad Bhagavad Gita, the destroyer of the illusion of manifestation Maya (Samsara), let's begin...

BHAGAVAD GITA VOLUME – 2

Chapter 7

Jnana - Vijnana Yoga / The Nature of Spirit and The Spirit of Nature

Introduction to Chapter 7

Knowledge of the ultimate Truth, the goal of Spiritual Science, is discussed in detail in chapter 7 titled *Jnana Vijnana* Yoga.

In this chapter we receive knowledge of the absolute reality. The Supreme Lord Krishna describes His illusory energy, Maya, and declares how difficult it is to overcome it.

This chapter is also referred to as union with the scientific knowledge or *jnana-vijnana-yoga* wherein the word *jnana* indicates supreme knowledge that culminates in wisdom; and *vijnana* indicates that this science is so logical and complete that there is no possibility of any modicum of doubt.

The next six chapters give us a detailed understanding of Tat as the Supreme Consciousness in Creation (Ishvara), and Sat as the Supreme Consciousness beyond Creation (Brahman).

The journey of the *jivatman*, the individual self, to become part of the Supreme Consciousness or *Param atman*, is either through Bhakti Yoga, Gyan Yoga, Karma Yoga or Raj Yoga. Depending on our tendencies, we can choose the path most suited to our Gunas. Bhakti Yoga is easier for most people, whereas the other paths require a lot of discipline [Sadhana].

Bhakti Yoga is discussed in detail in these chapters, as the path of utter devotion, surrender and worship, to merge with Supreme Consciousness and attain Moksha.

These chapters reveal the in-depth understanding of the terms Divinity, Cosmic Intelligence, Cosmic Consciousness, *Jiva atman, Uttam Purusha* and *Param atman.*

07

Jnana - Vijnana Yoga / The Nature of Spirit and The Spirit of Nature

<u>7.1</u>

Srī Bhagavān uvāca:
mayy āsaktamanāḥ pārtha yogaṁ yuñjan madāśrayaḥ |
asaṁśayaṁ samagraṁ māṁ yathā jñāsyasi tac chṛṇu ||

The Blessed Supreme said:

O Partha (Arjuna), absorbing thy mind in Me, taking shelter in Me, and following the path of

yoga-hear how thou shalt realize Me beyond all doubts, in full completion (knowing Me with all My attributes and powers)

<u>Explanation:</u>

How can we realize Him (the *Param Atman*)? How do we realize that complete knowledge that is to be known and realized. The Bhagavad Gita is the resource that moves us to realize that the Source (Brahman) is within and always has been within us. How can we achieve this total Union and alignment?

Krishna is getting ready to reveal the secret, esoteric knowledge of creation to Arjuna.

<u>Esoteric Explanation:</u>

Only the very selected few can receive and realize the value of this secret knowledge. Lord Krishna finds Arjuna a suitable candidate to receive the supreme secret now, after having prepared him in the previous six chapters.

The underlying message here is that one may not "hear" the voice of the spirit unless we humbly become seekers of this revered knowledge and open ourselves to receive it in humility, surrender and reverence.

21

7.2

jñānaṁ te 'haṁ savijñānam idaṁ vakṣyāmy aśeṣataḥ |
yaj jñātvā neha bhūyo 'nyaj jñātavyam avaśiṣyate ||

I shall relate to thee without omission both theoretical wisdom and that wisdom which can be known only by intuitive realisation, knowing which, naught in this world will remain unknown to thee.

Explanation:

Without omitting any vital information, Krishna says, "I will tell you, both the theoretical and the intuitive knowledge that will convert you into a *Jnani* or Knower of all that is to be known.

He says that this knowledge [7.1] referred to by the words *idam jnanam,* meaning, the theoretical knowledge as described in the Vedic scriptures and *sa-vijnanam* meaning knowledge, backed by Science based on realisation, will be revealed to the seeker.

The combination of theoretical knowledge and realisation from one's very own actual experience ensures that there will be nothing else to be known for a seeker in this world in order to attain *moksha* from the material existence. The one who is engaged in practicing *yoga* (the science of the individual consciousness attaining communion with the ultimate consciousness) becomes realized.

Even though this transcendental knowledge is a secret, Krishna reveals it to His devotee, starting with the revelation of His superior and inferior nature:

Esoteric Explanation:

He as *Purusha,* is eternal in the form of the *Atman*, Soul or Spirit and is simultaneously and distinctly different from both his higher and lower natures. *Purusha* is the *atman* or soul within all conscious beings and that which sustains the whole universe.

His higher nature is *para* (higher) prakriti before manifestation and His lower nature - *apara* (lower) prakriti/*maya* after manifestation and all her material products.

The lower aspect of *prakriti* is inferior as it is inert. It cannot subsist without the higher prakriti. Both higher and lower natures (*prakriti*) manifest from the Supreme Consciousness.

Brahman	Supreme Consciousness beyond Manifestation
Ishvara	Supreme Consciousness in Manifestation.
Para Prakriti	Higher Nature before manifestation
Apara Prakriti	Lower Nature after manifestation, physical universe.

Chart 2

The ancient scripture *Vishnu Purana* states that although the individual *atman* (*jivatman*) is part of the *Paramatman,* it is still understood to be subservient to the Supreme.

Brahman alone is the sole source of the entire creation and can dissolve it as well, by only a fraction of His will. He is the cause of the creation of the inanimate temporary physical body, and He is the cause of the animate eternal embodied *atman* or soul. The physical body cannot sustain and grow without the life principle of the *atman* and both the physical body, and the soul are His powers and completely under His control.

Brahman is paramount and superior to everything with nothing existing beyond Him and nothing that exists is separate from Him. There is no supernatural, or any other being in existence that possesses even a fraction of His attributes and qualities, nor does any being have the competency to imitate His cosmic potencies.

7.3

> manuṣyāṇāṁ sahasreṣu kaścid yatati siddhaye |
> yatatām api siddhānāṁ kaścin māṁ vetti tattvataḥ ||

Among thousands of men, perhaps one strives for spiritual attainment; and, among the blessed true seekers that assiduously try to reach Me, perhaps one perceives Me as I am.

Explanation:

Amongst all the men very few strive for spirituality and then amongst the ones who try to attain knowledge, only few reach this pinnacle. This knowledge is very difficult to obtain and without devotion to the Supreme Source, transcendental knowledge about Him is impossible to understand. Only humans, who have the highest level of consciousness, have the required qualifications for *moksha*. Only when one has gained *antahakaran shuddhi* (self-purification) can one attempt to commune with the divine source.

Among the thousands of humans only some due to great merit ever attempt to gain *moksha* and among the hundreds of thousands who try for *moksha,* only few will achieve it due to extraordinary activities continuing on from previous births.

7.4

bhūmir āpo 'nalo vāyuḥ khaṁ mano buddhir eva ca |
ahaṁkāra itīyaṁ me bhinnā prakṛtir aṣṭadhā ||

My manifested nature (Prakriti) has an eightfold differentiation: earth, water, fire, air, ether, sensory mind (manas), intelligence (buddhi), and egoism (ahamkara).

Explanation:

Brahman, the Supreme Consciousness, the unmanifested field of unlimited potential decides to manifest the world.

That aspect of Brahman that creates is Ishvara or Kutastha Chaitanya. His very nature is Para Prakriti, the infinite timeless power of the self-existent being out of which all existence in the cosmos are manifested. His lower nature is the Apara prakriti, when manifested, and is the material cause of this world. [See creation chart at the end of the book.]

The following are the five subtle elements *tanmatras*, from which the gross elements are created:

Tan Matras	Subtle Elements		Maha Bhuta
Shabd	Sound	*Akash*	Ether
Sparsh	Touch	*Vayu*	Air
Roop	Form, Sight	*Agni*	Fire
Ras	Taste	*Jal, Apaha*	Water
Gandh	Smell	*Bhumi, Prithvi*	Earth

Chart 3

The *Panch Mahabhutas* are the gross evolutes of *Prakriti*, and the material world is made up of these elements. The *tanmatras* are the most subtle. They are more independent, more pervasive and less perceivable. As vibration decreases, the subtlety decreases, and the five elements evolve.

[See chart at end of book]

Prakriti is Brahman's manifested nature, Its eightfold differentiation:

Apara Prakriti consists of:	*Tan Matras* from which emerge *the 5 Mahabhuta's*	*5 Maha Bhuta and antahakaran*
5 main elements	Sound, Touch, Sight, Taste Smell	Ether, Air, Fire, Water, Earth
3 elements of Antahakarana	Ego, Intellect, the Mind	*Ahamkara, Buddhi, Manas*

Chart 4A

The sages counted 24 factors that constitute the manifested creation:				
The four (4) [thought modifications]	The five (5) great elements [panch mahabhutas]	The five (5) organs of perception [panch gyana indriyas]	the five (5) organs of action [panch karma indriyas]	The five (5) Pranas that control the processes of [metabolism, elimination, crystallization, assimilation & circulation]
Chitta, Ahamkara, Buddhi, Manas	**Ether, Air, Fire, Water & Earth**	**Ears, Skin, Eyes, Tongue, Nose**	**Mouth, Hands, Feet, Genitalia, Anus**	**Prana, apana, vyana, samana, udana**

Chart 4B

7.5

apareyam itas tv anyāṁ prakṛtiṁ viddhi me parām |
jīvabhūtāṁ mahābāho yayedaṁ dhāryate jagat ||

Thus, My lower nature (Apara-Prakriti). But understand, O mighty armed (Arjuna) that, my different and higher nature (Para-Prakriti) is the jiva, the self-consciousness and life principle that sustains the cosmos.

Explanation:

He says that his lower nature as matter is the apara prakriti. and the higher nature as *jiva* [para-prakriti] is the consciousness of the Soul, the life principle that sustains the world.

The divine power of **Ishvara**, which makes matter take form, is called Maya.

Before manifestation prakriti is para-prakriti. When manifested prakriti is apara prakriti.

Para Prakriti is beyond and bigger than all the five senses, *Manas, Buddhi & Ahamkara.*

At the Microcosmic level, the individual consciousness, *jivatman*, is attached with its manifested or incarnate state and operates as an individualized entity, though it is the image of the divine.

On the Macrocosmic level, *Kutastha Chaitanya* or *Param atman,* is immanent in all creation as the unchanging pure reflection of the Soul of the Universe.

Brahman beyond Creation	***Brahman***
Brahman in Creation	*Kutastha Chaitanya* (**Ishvara** in creation)
Brahman the intelligent cosmic nature	*Para and Apara Prakriti* (unmanifest and manifest creation)

Chart 5

The reference for the great elements and their evolutes, creation, descent of man into substantiality and the effect of gunas (natures triune properties) is also detailed in the charts at the end of the book

CHART OF CREATION

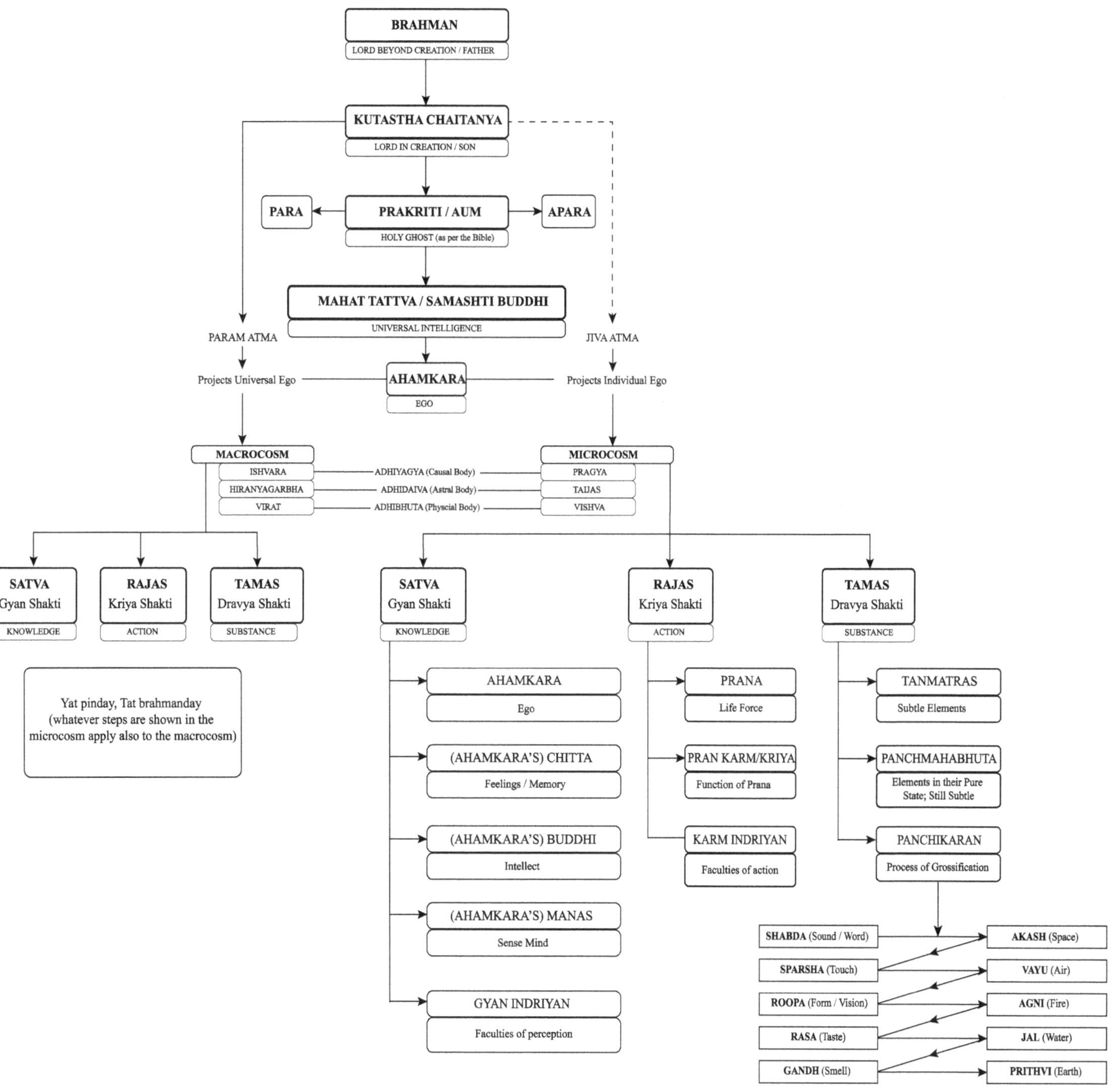

Brahman-Spirit	Ishvara	Prakriti-Matter
Sat	*Tat*	*Om*
Nirgun **Brahman**	*Sagun* **Brahman**	
Unmanifest Supreme Consciousness or Brahman without any attributes or form.	Brahman in its manifested state, with attributes or also as the conditioned Brahman, the supreme Ishvara of this universe.	Creative energy, with himself as Spirit, He reveals the other side of Himself, the total ***mool prakriti*** or the root of all matter.
Jagat karan	*Nimit karan* or the intelligent cause	*Upadan karan* or the material cause
There is one infinite, eternal, formless, changeless existence. One vibrationless, cosmic intelligence. Before creation/time/space evolved, Is Brahman.		Prakriti, matter is that which takes form and so can give bodies all sorts of shapes and kinds. It is dualistic, trigunatmika and subject to change.
From that all comes forth and into that all returns.		The universe is a manifestation of Brahman
That is all that ever has been, all that ever is and all that will ever be.		All that we can taste, touch, smell, see and hear is matter and a great deal more which our five senses are not yet developed to perceive
In Sanatana Dharma, this existence [sat], consciousness [chit], bliss [anand] is called Brahman=Sat	Kutastha Chaitanya Purushuttam, Ishvara or Creative Intelligence, Tat.	Prakriti, Mool prakriti Om - creative energy.
It is the Knower		It is the object of Knowledge

Chart 6

7.6

etadyonīni bhūtāni sarvāṇīty upadhāraya |
ahaṁ kṛtsnasya jagatah prabhavaḥ pralayas tathā ||

Understand that these dual Natures of Mine, the pure and the impure Prakriti, are the womb of all beings. I am the Progenitor and the Dissolver of the entire cosmos.

Esoteric Explanation:

Krishna describes the dual nature of His *Prakriti*.

All things, animate or inanimate, have the two *prakriti's* as their origin - cause and are included in one of these two *prakriti*'s, being either *kshetra* the field of activity or *kshetrajna* the utilizer and knower of the field of activity. Of these the inert lower nature evolves as a physical body.

Whereas the conscious *Jiva* having the eternal spark from the Supreme source, being the *atman* or soul, resides in all sentient beings as the witness and experiencer and sustains each being.

Ishvara is the progenitor and the dissolver of the cosmos.

The **Gross Body** is that which is made up of the 5 great elements that have undergone the process of *panchikarana,* born as a result of the good actions of the past, and is the counter of experiences like joy, sorrow and so on and subject to six modifications, *shad-vikaras* namely: to exist, to be born, to grow, to mature, to decay and to die.

The **Subtle body** is that which is composed of the five great elements which have not undergone grossification. It is an instrument for the experience of joy, sorrow, and so on, constituted of the 19 items [the 5 sense organs, the 5 organs of action, the five pranas, the mind, intellect, ego and consciousness]. Pervading the gross body is the subtle body. It is also subject to the *Shad-Vikaras*; hence it is a Body.

The **Causal Body** is that which is inexplicable, beginningless, in the form of ignorance, the sole cause of the two bodies [gross and subtle], ignorant of one's true nature, free from duality. it is the subtlest of the three bodies and pervades the other two. It is also subject to the shad-vikaras, it dies when the *jivatman* unites with the *Paramatman*, hence is a body. **(taken from the study of *Tatvabodh*)**

All three bodies (gross, subtle and causal) are considered as matter in the microcosm (*jivatman*). Also, the gross world, the subtle world and the causal world are considered as matter in the macrocosm (the Universe).

Refer to Illustration A at the end of the book

The Soul or the *Atman,* is the experiencer, the knower, which never dies. It is free of the modifications of the body, hence is the **Spirit.** That which is subject to change and is impermanent is **matter.** Anything other than Atman is **object.** Atman is the eternal **subject**, unchanging.

Spirit – *Purusha*	Matter - *Prakriti*
Infinite	Finite
Spirt cannot be perceived	Matter can be perceived
It is formless	It takes form, it has the tendency to be constantly dividing and changing forms
It is the same in everybody	It keeps changing
Spirit is the Knower	Matter is the Known. It is the object of Knowledge
The nature of Spirit is *Sat, Chit, Ananda*	The nature of *prakriti* is duality and trigunatmika [*Satva, Rajas, Tamas]*

Chart 7

The Modifications undergone by a body: The *Shad Vikaras*

Asti	To exist
Jayate	To be born
Vardhate	To grow
Viparinamate	To mature
Apakshiyate	To decay
Vinasyati	To die

Chart 8

7.7

mattaḥ parataraṁ nānyat kiṁcid asti dhanaṁjaya |
mayi sarvam idaṁ protaṁ sūtre maṇigaṇā iva ||

O Arjuna! There is nothing higher than Me, or beyond Me. All things (creatures and objects) are bound to Me like a row of gems on a thread.

Explanation:

Like the thread in a pearl necklace, everything is Me and bound to me. Indeed, the Vishva is my extension, my body. Brahman - Infinite, Causeless and Eternal. Beginning less, ever existent, ever conscious and self-evolved. Omnipresent, Omniscient and Omnipotent. Everything that is finite is contained within this infinite and threaded together by divine consciousness.

In this verse it is explained that the commonality of man is strung together by the spirit of Consciousness or Brahman. So even though human individuality makes us believe in the differences between one and the other, Krishna wants us to know that we are all one and that it is the same consciousness that runs through every soul.

The mind, the intellect and the body also work together in harmony and are held together by the Spirit. The infinite sky of the Spirit contains in it, all the finite manifestations of creation. Naught or nothing is beyond the infinite.

This "I" in this verse is *Purusha*, the Spirit that enlivens matter, the energy which gives motion to the atom, the vivifying of matter which would remain inert without *prana*.

7.8

raso 'ham apsu kaunteya prabhā 'smi śaśisūryayoḥ |
praṇavaḥ sarvavedeṣu śabdaḥ khe pauruṣaṁ nṛṣu ||

O Son of Kunti (Arjuna), I am the fluidity in waters; I am the radiation in the moon and the sun; I am the Aum (pranava) in all the Vedas; the sound in the ether; and the manliness in men.

Explanation:

Here He explains that He is the essence in all of creation. The very life in all beings and the Dharma or very nature of each substance. He is the Om (*pranava*) in the *Vedas*. The vibration in ether or space and the fluidity of water. The common man can only see a finite Creation and his vision usually cannot fathom infinity. A yogi can begin to intuitively fathom cosmic sound, cosmic light, and cosmic consciousness. He can expand beyond the vision of dreams (Maya) and reach beyond this earthly plane.

7.9

> puṇyo gandhaḥ pṛthivyāṁ ca tejaś cāsmi vibhāvasau |
> jīvanaṁ sarvabhūteṣu tapaś cāsmi tapasviṣu ||

I am the wholesome fragrance exuding from the earth; the luminescence in the fire am I; the life in all creatures, and the self-discipline in anchorites. (He who lives in seclusion)

Explanation:

In all these verses Krishna explains to Arjuna the power of the Supreme. In every verse that follows, he elaborates, using various similes and metaphors, and describes the connection between Creation, the Consciousness, the Universe, and Infinity.

The ultimate meanings derived from these verses is that Ishvara made man in his image.

Then he added free will and the power of discrimination to man. After this, he left mankind to sort themselves out by trying to emerge out of the entanglements of Maya, that he had so carefully planned for us as an experience.

He did this so that we could learn to enjoy the world, without getting attached to it, rise / transcend above and strive to realize our full potential as the incarnate of the Divine. Man must learn to pull himself up and away from all sensory traps.

Esoteric Meaning:

Our life force must be lifted within the spine from the lower to the upper regions through meditation and discipline via raising our vibrational energies through the chakras. Chakras are the seven subtle or astral centers of vibrational energies, along the astral spine. These regulate our lives, and the techniques used to balance and energize them are also known as the science of Raja Yoga.

Here the yogi can experience divinity and its nature in the cerebrospinal centers.

He says I am: In the coccygeal center - the fragrance from the earth, in the lumbar center - the light of fire, in the dorsal center - the very life in all creatures and in the cerebral center - the discipline in religious recluses.

7.10

bījaṁ māṁ sarvabhūtānāṁ viddhi pārtha sanātanam |
buddhir buddhimatām asmi tejas tejasvinām aham ||

Know Me to be the eternal seed of all creatures, O Son of Pritha (Arjuna)! I am the understanding of the keen, the radiance of vital beings.

Explanation:

I am the seed of all beings, living and non-living. I am the intelligence of the intelligent, the power of discrimination within you, and the glory of the glorious. Intelligence, strength, radiance, power, beauty and brilliance, all derive their source from Him.

7.11

balaṁ balavatāṁ cāhaṁ kāmarāgavivarjitam |
dharmāviruddho bhūteṣu kāmo 'smi bharatarṣabha ||

Among the powerful, O Best of the Bharatas (Arjuna), I am the power that is free from longings and attachment. I am that desire in men which is in keeping with dharma (righteousness).

Explanation:

He is the strength of the strong, free from passion and desire and the desire unopposed to Dharma (not conflicting with virtue). In harmony. How can the limited limit the limitless? How can infinity be contained? Why does Man strive for goodness? This is the desire that is created in Man in keeping with the righteous way of living.

7.12

ye caiva sāttvikā bhāvā rājasās tāmasāś ca ye |
matta eveti tān viddhi na tv ahaṁ teṣu te mayi ||

Know thou that all manifestations of satva (good), rajas (activity), and tamas (evil) emanate from Me. Though they are in Me, I am not in them.

Explanation:

Man acts under the influence of *Maya* with which he is helplessly bound. *Prakriti* or *Maya* is *trigunatmika*. The three *Gunas*: *Satva* [the knowledge factor] Rajas [Activity], and *Tamas* [inertia) are intrinsic to all of Creation. *Gunas*, as they are known, if understood can help in Man's quest to become exalted. Though everything emanates from the Source, evolves from Him, he is not in them.

"Although all Gunas emanate from me I am not in them".

As everything is Him but each aspect is differentiated so the totality of the Divine source is not in the *Gunas*. He is free of the Gunas, Nirguna, unlike Prakriti.

7.13

tribhir guṇamayair bhāvair ebhiḥ sarvam idaṁ jagat |
mohitaṁ nābhijānāti mām ebhyaḥ param avyayam ||

This world of mortal beings does not perceive Me, unchangeable and beyond all qualities, because they are deluded by the triple modes of Nature.

Explanation:

Avyaya means that which does not die and also that which is not born (*vyaya* means - death and all that is taking place between birth and death.

We are deluded by the 3 Gunas of Nature – ***Satva Rajas Tamas***

Satva Rajas Tamas are the triple modes of nature and are the operating principles or tendencies of all beings and in everything that is created in this universe. A Yogi must transcend all the three gunas to merge with the Source.

***Maya* itself is an interplay of:**

Satva	Goodness	Purity	Calmness and Wisdom
Rajas	Passion	Activity and Ego	Doership
Tamas	Imbalance, delusion and ignorance	Dissolution and Destruction	Inertia for stopping and also needed for sleep and rest

Chart 9

Satva	Rajas	Tamas
Knowledge	**Action**	**Substantiality**
Jnana Shakti	***Kriya Shakti***	***Dravya Shakti***
Balance	Movement	Inertia
Harmony	Activity	Inactivity
Positive	Energy	Negativity
Peace	Excitement	Dullness
Wisdom	Passion	Apathy

Chart 10

The three modes or *Gunas* (modes of nature) are:	
Satva	Anything noble, pure and inclusive
Rajas	Ambitious, highly active, with raga dvesa, and attachments
Tamas	Delusion, ignorance, false values, inactivity

Chart 11

Under these three different impulses, the mind and intellect works. These three are eternal modes of our subtle body. These 3 are the qualities of the *antahakaran*. Man does not know the Supreme source because of delusion, false ego, lack of discrimination about the eternal and non-eternal (*sat and asat*). He is incapable of knowing his true nature as he is deluded by the gunas.

Yoga maya means *Maya* united with the 3 gunas (*Satva, Rajas and Tamas*) A person does not know that I am the one who is unborn and changeless. People are deluded and do not recognize me. There is only one thing in this world that can be deluded and that is the Mind (not *atman* or consciousness). All delusion resides there. The consciousness conditioned by the mind does not know me. The intellect veiled by maya amounts to this.

The obstruction is not in the atman, it is in the mind where the knowledge must dawn. Therefore, we say that there is ignorance in the mind until knowledge dawns.

Ishvara like a magician, casts a spell on us, but He never comes under the same spell.

7.14

daivī hy eṣā guṇamayī mama māyā duratyayā |
mām eva ye prapadyante māyām etāṁ taranti te ||

It is difficult indeed to go beyond the influence of My divine cosmic hypnosis, imbued with the triple qualities. Only those who take shelter in Me (the Cosmic Hypnotizer) become free from this power of illusion.

Explanation:

The Supreme is a cosmic hypnotizer. We are hypnotized by the attraction of material nature.

The hypnotic process occurs as our sensory searchlights are directed to the outer world. So how do we free ourselves from the hypnotic spell of the world out there – Maya is mesmerizing! And we are like puppets in her mesmerizing world of duality and pairs of opposites.

Animals cannot turn their search light inward as they are governed by instinct, but we, only Human beings, have the free will choice and the discriminative choice making ability to do so. As we can cultivate a rest-fullness within us, we do not have to react instinctively or be habit bound.

There is a lovely story of Vishnu and Sage Narada. It illustrates how beautifully the world, with its family and children lure can keep us trapped forever. Even Lord Vishnu had to be extracted from this blissful attachment to Maya when he incarnated into a pregnant sow.

Knowing he may get trapped, he pre-arranged for Narada to extricate him from his incarnation as a sow, in case he forgot his own true nature.

Although it is difficult to overcome the divine magnetism of material nature, one who surrenders and takes refuge in *Atman* can overcome this illusion. The controller of maya is Brahman, so by single pointed devotion, the mind can contemplate upon the self. Through study and concentrated practice one can overcome the trappings of *maya.*

7.15

na māṁ duṣkṛtino mūḍhāḥ prapadyante narādhamāḥ |
māyayāpahṛtajñānā āsuraṁ bhāvam āśritāḥ ||

The lowest of men, perpetrators of evil and misguided fools, whose discrimination has been stolen by maya (delusion), follow the path of demoniac beings, failing to take shelter in Me.

Explanation:

In Tamas, discriminative power is lost in veils of ignorance and delusion. Not recognizing their true nature and potential, the deluded are attracted by the material world and spend their life pursuing temporary pleasures and material gains, employing wrongful and evil ways. Evil is anything that does not cause upliftment. Evil is that which causes misery to the evil person and to those around him.

The four types of people who <u>do not</u> seek true knowledge are:

Mudhaha	those who are deluded by *Maya*
Naradhama	lowest among human, no religious principle
Apahrta Jnana	those who have lost their *viveka* (wisdom)
Asura Bhava	those who have demonic proclivities

Chart 12

7.16

caturvidhā bhajante māṁ janāḥ sukṛtino 'rjuna |
ārtho jijñāsur arthārthī jñānī ca bharataṛṣabha ||

The afflicted, the questers for wisdom, the cravers for power here and in the hereafter, and the wise, these O Arjuna, are the four kinds of righteous men who pursue Me.

Explanation:

Seekers of spiritual wisdom eventually find Me.

He describes four types of devotees, people attracted to divinity and the four types of people who are opposed to divinity.

Only those who are virtuous and righteous have the qualification for devotion to the Supreme.

There are four categories of such qualified beings according to the differences in their virtue.

Those who perform virtuous deeds in previous lives worship Krishna and fall into four categories:

*1) **Artho*** (those who are distressed)

Those that are suffering and are in pain. They only want to alleviate their sorrow and misery.

Arthos are those distressed and persecuted by disease and poverty. If they performed virtuous activities in past lives, then they will have the opportunity to worship Krishna otherwise they will be limited to worshipping minor devas and formless illusionary beings.

Arthos are those impoverished and distressed beings, who after losing all wealth and power, desire that the Devatas recover these for them and re-instate them to glory.

Arthos are those afflicted by problems such as disease or enemies. If one has enough accumulated merit, then they will have the opportunity to worship the Supreme to alleviate their distress.

Artho means materialistic, the one who calls or remembers God only when he is in distress.

*2) **Artharthi*** (those who want material pleasures and gain)

Those who seek utter fulfilment including wealth, health, power and spiritual prowess.

In a balanced way they are also seeking a good life along with divine realisation.

Artharthis are the seekers of wealth who desire to have full facility for enjoyment in this life and their next. If they performed virtuous deeds in their past lives, then they too will have the opportunity to worship Krishna.

Artharthis are those seekers of wealth who desire to regain their position of power and enjoyments which they had before and perhaps are now deprived of.

Artharthis remember God for the fulfilment of worldly desires and are also known as *kamya karmi's,* who perform actions with a desire to accomplish goals within the material world. They seek complete fulfilment including wealth, health, power and spiritual prowess, in a balanced manner and are also seeking a good life along with divine Realisation. *Artho's* and *Artharthi's* are both *Karmi's*

3) *Jigyasu* (those that are the inquisitive, seeking self-realisation)

Those who seek wisdom to solve the mystery of life. Using their free will choice to do good.

Jigyasus are those who desire self-Realisation to end the cycle of birth and death.

Jigyasus are the seekers of self-Realisation who are anxious to know the *atman* or soul in its real state, separate from matter for the benefit of escaping transmigration [the cycle of birth and death] and pray to the Supreme for benediction to discover this. They are liberation seekers who also have enough acquired merit from previous lives to qualify for worship of the Supreme.

Jigyasus are the ones who want to know Ishvara with keen curiosity. They invoke the grace of Spirit in order to gain a clear mind for understanding the knowledge of Self. The *Jigyasu* is on the path of *Karma Yoga.*

Artho's, Artharthi's and Jigyasu's are not strictly pure devotees because they have some aspirations to fulfil in exchange of their devotional service. Their devotion is transactional.

4) *Jnani's* (*Jnana*) are those who are learned and wise. They are *viveki's* who have achieved *atman bodh.* The Sages, the Yogis, the Gurus are the greatest of them all. Their goal is not just the acquisition of knowledge, nor do they seek Union for the fulfilment of desires.

Jnani's are those who have achieved *atman gyana* or Realisation of the soul and know the Supreme and recognize the truth completely.

If they have performed virtuous activities in their past lives, then they will have the opportunity of advancing further and worshipping their Lord.

Jnani's are the seekers of knowledge concerning the Supreme who realize that the *atman* is essentially characterized by its being an eternal ingredient of the Supreme residing within all embodied beings. Such a one considers the Supreme as their goal of life and attainment of Him the fulfilment of all ambitions.

Jnani's or those of spiritual wisdom who have no selfish motives and are endowed with discriminative intelligence from ascertaining the reality of the *atman* or soul and its relationship as an eternal part of the Supreme. They also achieve *moksha,* as they continue to worship the Supreme.

Although *artho's, artharthi's and jignasuh's* are all devotees, it is the *jnani's* devotional service that is considered pure. *Jnani's* only purpose is to serve our creation with awe, love and devotion.

Pure devotional service is without any desire. The Self is the source of all existence and energy. To fulfil egocentric requirements through our mind, body, and intellect we need to invoke the required energy from pure Consciousness. This invocation requires energy to procure a concentrated flow into the channel of prayers or *jaap.* In all sincere prayers, the ego surrenders itself to the Spirit in the quest for liberation.

There are 2 types of actions
1.Gives material pleasure and does not require any spiritual or inner growth
2. That which is purely spiritual

<u>Chart 13</u>

<u>7.17-18</u>

tesāṁ jñānī nityayukta ekabhaktir viśiṣyate |
priyo hi jñānino'tyartham ahaṁ sa ca mama priyaḥ ||
udārāḥ sarva evaite jñānī tv ātmaiva me matam |
āsthitaḥ sa hi yuktātmā mām evānuttamāṁ gatim ||

Chief among them is the sage, ever constant and one-pointed in devotion. For I am exceedingly dear to the sage, and he is exceedingly dear to Me.

All these (four kinds of men) are noble, but the sage I

consider indeed as My own Self. Unwaveringly is he settled in Me alone, as his utmost goal.

Explanation:

All seekers are noble but the chief amongst all is the Yogi Sage who is most dear to me. Instead of seeking worldly gifts the Yogi seeks this Union – He is the seeker of the Self.

7.19

bahūnāṁ janmanām ante jñānavān māṁ prapadyate |
vāsudevaḥ sarvam iti sa mahātmā sudurlabhaḥ ||

After many incarnations, the sage attains Me, realizing, "The Supreme is all-pervading!" A man so illumined is hard to find.

Explanation:

Depending on intensity of practice our spiritual journey can be completed in 6, 12, 24 or 48 years. Or it can take many lifetimes depending on the discriminative choices we make. It is our choice alone that can lead us back to the source!

The Supreme is not to be earned as his essence is already intrinsic in us as the Atman. We only need to rediscover this blissful spirit and align with the divine. The Spirit remains unaffected as an observer witness, whilst we get caught up due to the *Gunas* and get lost in this world and its gameplay.

This verse does not require us to love the controller who is in heaven, nor that we pray or bow down in Bhakti to an entity outside of us. God resides within us hence self-realisation is the key.

This verse explains that we have infinite power of Love and that is all we must give. Love of Nature - Love of Mankind - Love of Creation and most importantly Self-Love. Self-Realisation is Self-Love.

Krishna continues to talk about the *jnani*, who out of the four types of devotees, is the most exalted and closest to becoming all knowing.

<u>Esoteric Explanation:</u>

Many astrologers and ancient gurus have stated that the above verse 7.19 determines where the soul would rest at death, as per the time and season when death occurs.

As per Paramhansa Yogananda's teaching if a human dies when he is in personal spiritual ascent into knowledge or descent into sensory world that then determines his next birth.

A Sage realizes the Self after many reincarnations and is hard to find.

Describing the concept of Raja Yoga. Every day we wake up and then we die - we have an average of 27,000 days and 27,000 nights in 75 years. Each Day and each night are a chance for us to jump one Birth.

Sages know how to do this and try to balance their karma in this one lifetime, so they don't remain in the cycle of birth and death for too long.

An understanding of our life and play of the mind which has 60,000 thoughts per day can be achieved through **Tapas.**

Tapas is austerity of body, speech and mind carried out to achieve power of purification. This verse also says that it is very rare to find a person, whose mind at the end of many births, is mature enough to gain this knowledge and seek *Jnana*.

He is a *Jnani* who understands *Ishvara* alone is everything, He understands the identity between the 'I' of Jiva and the 'I' of *Ishvara* and sees that all is Ishvara. He knows that the only truth is Atman, which is Brahman.

Ishvara is the one in whom everything exists, by whom everything is sustained. It causes everything to exist and is the basis of every existence). Its own nature is pure consciousness.

7.20

kāmais tais tair hṛtajñānāh prapadyante 'nyadevatāḥ |
taṁ taṁ niyamam āsthāya prakṛtyā niyatāḥ svayā ||

Led by their own inclinations, their discrimination stolen by this or that craving, pursuing this or that cultic injunction, men seek lesser devatas.

<u>Explanation:</u>

This verse says, people who are devoid of wisdom seek other deities for various desires like wealth, child, power, fame etc. Because of these desires, the power of discrimination is lost. To fulfil these desires, they also observe certain practices like offer prayers to invoke a specific deva (demigod) for a specific result. Praying to lesser Gods (minor devas, yakshas or angels) reaps limited results.

For gaining the ultimate vision, we must overcome desires and pursue the understanding of *Atman.* And for that, we must have *viveka* [discrimination].

Every human being is an incarnation and has the potential to be the full projection of the source. *"Aham Brahmasmi"*

Every human being is on a different stage of spiritual evolvement. The higher we evolve, the more powerful our *siddhis* or prowess's become.

Every form of worship, in whatever form of worship reaches the Source of worship, Supreme Consciousness.

No matter if it's Kali, Shiva, Krishna, Sarasvati, Lakshmi, or Durga as the deity - sincere devotion is always to the source.

7.21-22

yo yo yāṁ yāṁ tanuṁ bhaktaḥ śraddhayārcitum icchati |
tasya tasyācalāṁ śraddhāṁ tām eva vidadhāmy aham ||

sa tayā śraddhayā yuktas tasyārādhanam īhate |
labhate ca tataḥ kāmān mayaiva vihitān hi tān ||

Whatever embodiment (a Brahmin-incarnate, a saint, or a deity) a devotee strives faithfully to worship, it is I who make his devotion unflinching.

Absorbed in that devotion, intent on the worship of that embodiment, the devotee thus gains the fruits of his longings. Yet those fulfilments are verily granted by Me alone.

Explanation:

Resolute *Dharana and Dhyana* comes with discipline. The source of this is always the Self. In whichever form the devotees worship these Gods, in that form the cosmos blesses them.

By giving devotees their desired results, it makes their faith firm in their respective devata. These results are determined by Krishna himself, but devotees think that wishes are being granted by their devata. This goes on, till the devotee reaches a level of maturity and understanding.

The minor incarnations of divinity reside in Swarga Lok or the Astral world and can grant favors or could be compared to departmental heads. The Devis and Devas (demigods) are like project heads who have been assigned certain responsibilities of granting limited favors and desire gratification.

7.23

> antavat tu phalaṁ teṣāṁ tad bhavaty alpamedhasām |
> devān devayajo yānti madbhaktā yānti mām api ||

But men of scant knowledge (worshipping lesser gods) receive limited results. The devotees of the deities go unto them; My devotees come unto Me.

<u>Explanation:</u>

For all the followers of Bhakti Yog, this is the time to understand that Bhakti alone, without deep understanding, without knowledge and without the aligned dharmic actions necessary to make Bhakti blossom and fructify, will not result in our complete growth.

However, superficial seekers worship astral deities only for desire fulfilment. Their wishes are granted by <u>Grace</u> from the ultimate source of divinity.

Further, people with limited discrimination, who engage in venerating the lesser deities, get results which are finite. These results are temporary and will eventually come to an end.

Whereas devotees who worship *Brahman*, who have the knowledge of truth, attain Him. The result they achieve is *Moksha*, which is infinite.

Every religious philosophy has 2 components:

1. The wise way of living in this world is in accordance with *dharma* where gratification of desires are fulfilled ethically and actions are conducted in a *satvik* manner.

2. Another way is that which enables us to transcend *samsara* or the material world. This is the way to overcome suffering and attain liberation.

7.24

avyaktaṁ vyaktim āpannaṁ manyante mām abuddhayaḥ |
paraṁ bhāvam ajānanto mamāvyayam anuttamam ||

Men without wisdom consider Me, the Unmanifest, as assuming embodiment (like a mortal being taking a form)-not understanding My unsurpassable state, my unchangeable unutterable nature.

Explanation:

So, who is this Super Supreme - the One and only - the source of Creation "Brahman?"

Krishna says – "if you have the entire source within you, why pray for small favors and that too from lesser potentials of the divine source"?

Life and its experiences are just a drama. Observe the unfolding of life as a witness without attachment.

The ignorant see 'Him' only as an avatar of Vishnu, manifested as Krishna. They do not understand the real nature of Krishna, which is Sat, Chit, Ananda. He is atman of everyone and the whole world. We may think, Krishna is someone separate from ourselves and thus remain ignorant.

Whereas the wise know the 'Self' as Param atman, the formless, the changeless and infinite, the field of unlimited potential beyond which there is nothing left.

In next verse, Krishna, explains why are people unable to see his real nature?

7.25

nāhaṁ prakāśaḥ sarvasya yogamāyāsamāvṛtaḥ |
mūḍho 'yaṁ nābhijānāti loko mām ajam avyayam ||

Seemingly eclipsed by My own Yoga-Maya (the delusion born of the triple qualities in Nature), I am unseen by men. The bewildered world knows not Me, the Unborn, the Deathless.

<u>Explanation:</u>

My own Maya has eclipsed the understanding of men who know me not, the unborn and the deathless. Men are deluded by the three gunas of nature. They have lost their discriminative powers and are attached to their material existence. Hence they do not see the Eternal Truth.

7.26

> vedāhaṁ samatītāni vartamānāni cārjuna |
> bhaviṣyāṇi ca bhūtāni māṁ tu veda na kaścana ||

> **O Arjuna, I am aware of the creatures of the past, the present, and the future; but Me no one knows.**

<u>Explanation:</u>

Humans are limited by 3-fold relativity of time - Past, Present and Future.

What is Time? We usually forget the past, are aware of the present and unsure of our future. Sometimes we are also not able to escape the memories of the past, or we keep worrying about the future.

Krishna says - "As I am the basis of all conceptions of time - I know the beings of the past, present and future, nothing is hidden from my view, I am All-knowing"!

The obstructions caused by Maya are stated in the next verse.

7.27

> icchādveṣasamutthena dvandvamohena bhārata |
> sarvabhūtāni saṁmohaṁ sarge yānti paraṁtapa ||

> **O descendant of Bharata, scorcher of foes (Arjuna)! at birth all creatures are immersed in delusive ignorance (moha) by the delusion of the pairs of opposites springing from longing and aversion.**

Explanation:

Obstructed by maya we do not understand that maya does not exist apart from Brahman. It is relative and a mithya-delusion. Maya's reality is Brahman. Maya is created by Ishvara and Ishvara is Brahman, Cosmic Consciousness.

The main obstruction is delusion. Delusion is in the shape of pair of opposites. The pair of opposites are created by our own wishes and desires; Raga [attraction], and Dvesha, [repulsion]. Some opposites like hot or cold, day or night are created by Ishvara. Success or failure is viewed from our material, worldly standpoint.

The two enemies in the path of man's spiritual progress are declared under the names of *raga* or attractions and *dvesa* or aversions. The pair of opposites like joy and grief, pleasure and pain etc. which start from these two impulses are instrumental in tightening the hold of ignorance of Jiva – that is why these are called "delusion" *Maya-Mithya.*

Raga and dvesa also include anxiety and fear. Desires or *Raga* when not satisfied, produces anxiety and fear of losing what we are attached to. Dvesha on the other hand is a strong dislike bordering on hatred. These are powerful and do not allow us to see things as they are (people mistaking a rope for a snake). It is a veil that partially blinds the intellect and as a result things are not seen properly.

7.28

> yeṣāṁ tv antagataṁ pāpaṁ janānāṁ puṇyakarmaṇām |
> te dvandvamohanirmuktā bhajante māṁ dṛḍhavratāḥ ||

But righteous men, their sins obliterated, and subject no longer to the oppositional delusions, worship Me steadfastly.

Explanation:

In this verse, people who are freed from the pair of opposites, being firm in their commitment, seek *yuj* or union with the infinite, to cleanse their sinful nature by doing virtuous deeds.

They use their free will to do good deeds and refrain from bad deeds. They refuse to be under the spell of their likes and dislikes.

They are called *punya karmi's* (bringing joy) and the actions they do are done with selflessness for the common good.

These people are those for whom there is no longer a tendency to do wrong action.

The tendencies of wrongdoing cannot remain in us when we keep doing good. When we do any type of action repeatedly, it results in *samskara* (habits and tendencies). The more we do it, the more we reinforce a tendency for that type of action.

To break this pattern, one must use will power and discipline (*Manipura or Arjun chakra*)

It is usually hard to break a habit and is sometimes possible only by the grace of the Creator.

With determination and discipline, they become liberated from delusion of the opposites. These are the ones who recognize what is really sought in life and they worship Truth.

The journey to the divine awakening begins with the love of Brahman and culminates in the state of being one with Brahman.

True dharma is knowing ourselves as one with the divine.

7.29

> jarāmaraṇamokṣāya mām āśritya yatanti ye |
> te brahma tad viduḥ kṛtsnam adhyātmaṁ karma cākhilam ||
>
> **Those who seek deliverance from decay and death by clinging to Me know Brahman (the Absolute), the all-inclusiveness of Adhyatman (the soul as the repository of Spirit), and all secrets of karma.**

Explanation:

This is Advaita teaching - To reach oneness from Duality. From Dvait to Advaita. From looking for the divine outside of us to finding the divine source within – is Yog (union).

- Aum is the vibration that manifests into sound and light resulting in Creation.

- The absolute, all-inclusive Spirit is Brahman that which exists beyond the vibratory Aum.

The "Om" Vibration, emanating from Brahman, is the primordial sound accompanied by Cosmic Light. This is the vibration and cause of Creation.

Brahman's consciousness is what vibrates in our body as energy or Prana, and in death this is what leaves us in an instant. And yet, every breath we take, we forget that the power to breathe is not with us, it is just on loan along with this body for a short span of time of maybe 80-90 years if lucky enough.

7.30

sādhibhūtādhidaivaṁ māṁ sādhiyajñaṁ ca ye viduḥ |
prayāṇakāle 'pi ca māṁ te vidur yuktacetasaḥ ||

Those who perceive Me in the Adhi bhuta (the physical), the Adhidaiva (the astral), and the Adhiyajna (the spiritual), with heart united to the soul, continue to perceive Me even at the time of death.

Explanation:

Adhibhuta	centered on five elements / physical world and physical body
Adhidaiva	centered on Devas / astral world and astral body
Adhiyajna	centered on Yajnas / causal world and causal body
Adhyatma	centered on Brahman & Ishvara

Chart 14 (also Refer to Creation Chart after 7.6)

Having taken refuge in surrender to the Spirit *(Purusha),* those who make effort to free themselves, know the Truth.

They know the Lord as the master of all three worlds –

The Physical, The Astral and the Causal.

A person who is not under the spell of *raga-dvesa* has a mind that can discern this and seek a real solution. He understands the value of Yoga - Union in his life and seeks the *Paramatman* much before his impending old age and inevitable death.

If we perform regular sadhana - (disciplined practice of learning), it becomes a habit, and the seeking becomes ingrained in us. We can then remember Him and attain Him at the time of death.

This verse is a great lesson on "death" and how to prepare for the inevitable changing of body.

Mostly we are unprepared for death, and our ego enters a tug of war with death as desire of this physical life remains strong.

Delving into this knowledge helps in understanding the manifested true nature of the ego self, and ways to get over it. Rightful doer ship and renunciation of doer ship is the way forward.

Our body is a daily drama of activity. The mind with its sensory impressions and the discriminative intellect, gets emotionally agitated. We should keep the self away from this sway and prepare our self spiritually.

<u>Please refer to the Creation charts at the back of the book.</u>

<u>Summary of Chapter 7</u>

The Nature of Spirit and The Spirit of Nature

1. *Upanishads* describe Brahman as the cause of the universe – *Jagat Karan.*

2. Everything created requires a two-fold cause:

    Material cause – *Upadan Karan* and Intelligent cause – *Nimit Karan.*

3. *Upanishads* point out that Brahman alone existed before creation came into being.

4. There is one infinite, eternal, changeless existence. One vibrationless, cosmic intelligence. From that all comes forth and into that all returns. That has all that ever has been, is and will be.

5. In Sanatana Dharma, this Existence, Consciousness, Bliss is called Brahman.

6. The universe is a manifestation of Brahman. Various religions refer to the Creator with different names.

7. The Unmanifested Consciousness is called *Nirgun Brahman*, Brahman without attributes or form.

8. Brahman in its manifested state is called *Sagun Brahman*, with attributes or the conditioned Brahman, *Ishvara* with his universe.

9. Also sometimes referred to as *Uttam Purusha*, is the supreme Spirit, the Kutastha Chaitanya.

10. With himself as Spirit, *Ishvara / Purusha / Purusha uttam reveals* the other side of himself, the mool prakriti or the total root of all matter.

11. *Prakriti* or matter is that which takes form and so can give bodies all sorts of shapes and kinds. It is dualistic and trigunatmika (with three gunas). All that we can taste, touch, smell, see and hear is matter.

12. Knowing this difference between spirit and matter, to advance spiritually, we need to gradually learn to detach ourselves from matter and attach ourselves to our identity, that of the spirit.

13. Emancipation is a sum, composed of the yogis wholehearted effort, the guru's guidance and blessing and the grace of the divine source.

14. The way to acknowledge him and know him is by constantly keeping the attention absorbed in his holy vibration *Om*.

15. One who can thus absorb his mind into the Lord, even at the time of death, attains liberation.

Comments by nascent seekers of Vēdānta:

Spirit / *Purusha* [which is changeless and omnipotent] and matter / *prakriti* [which is forever changing and impermanent], come together in tandem, to create the manifested world.

When *Atman* is attached to the lower nature of prakriti, which is eightfold, made of *panch maha bhutas* [material body] and mind, intellect, ego [astral body], it is *Jiva Atman.*

When *Atman* is attached to *Purusha*, the Spirit, it is *Param Atman.*

Knowing this difference between spirit and matter, to advance spiritually, we need to gradually learn to detach ourselves from matter and attach ourselves to our identity, that of the spirit.

All problems are usually centered on the Ego. This problem of self-identity is what causes fear. With a mind absorbed in the Self, the mind, which was dwelling on the objects of *raga dvesa* will now start dwelling upon the Self. This will resolve many a misery of the mind.

By taking refuge, the devotee makes the effort to get close to Ishvara. The effort is for the sake of knowledge and that knowledge is freedom from the fear of old age and death.

People who take refuge in surrender, also understand the truth about *karma*. The truth about karma is that the doer, the object of action, the means of doing action, the purpose from where the action originates are all Ishvara.

The one who knows *Brahman* sees *Him* everywhere. Param Atman is telling us that there is no difference between Ishvara and Jiva.

Everything is *Bhagavan* or *Ishvara*. Therefore, those, whose minds do not have any inhibiting factors and know that all that is here is *Ishvara* need not even make an effort to think about him at the time of death. Those minds are already united with the cosmic consciousness. There is no return for such souls.

Those who know these five - *adhyatman, karma* in its entirety, *adhibhuta, adhidaiva* and *adhiyajna as Brahman,* for them their knowledge of the identity between themselves and Ishvara stands firm and unaffected even at the time of death.

Shallow seekers worship astral deities for desire fulfilment, but even then, the granter of wishes always remains "Karmic Grace" from the ultimate Source.

So, there is no doubt, that thoughts of desires are manifested into reality, and our Vedas are indeed full of promises, rituals etc. that work on precisely giving to man what he wants.

However, why do we need to beg, ask, request, plead to these managers of dreams when the manager of these dream managers is the ultimate? And the greatest irony is that the source of all this power is within and has always been within. Yet we continue to look outside. It is up to us.

We must overcome the *Vasana* (unfulfilled desires) which pull us into a multitude of births and death cycles. The causal body consists of vasanas which cause rebirth. Vasanas have to be transcended to find release from these cycles.

Practice of Kriya Yoga (Raja Yoga) allows us to evolve quickly and skip many incarnations and moves us rapidly towards Self-Realisation.

Even from the highest state of *samadhi* (when consciousness has merged with the primordial vibratory OM) we can sometimes revolve back into body consciousness of the Karan Sharira (Causal Body) which is persistent with desires and karmic bondages.

All worlds / lokas are subject to the finite law of recurrence (rebirth into finite body)

Man can only escape this law if he comes into "himself" or in other words merges into the absolute. (*Shoonya* or *Kevalya* which is only that - **Tat**)

Task 2 for reader: Examine the fears associated with death, for us and our loved ones.

Sat	Is the Absolute Truth, It Is nonexistence and existence itself. It is eternal and infinite and never changes
Tat	Is the undifferentiated and unmanifest Supreme Consciousness
Om	Creative energy resulting in manifestation

Chart 15

Om   Creative Vibration

Tat   Ishvara or Kutastha Chaitanya

Sat   Brahman

BHAGAVAD GITA VOLUME – 2

Chapter 8

The Imperishable Absolute / Akshara Brahma Yoga

Beyond the cycles of creation and dissolution

Introduction to Chapter 8

The aim of Vēdānta is to inspire ordinary people to realize their true potential, discard their attachment to their temporary identities and identify with their highest nature which is *Sat chit anand.*

This chapter begins with Arjuna asking 7 questions to Lord Krishna. He answers the first 6 questions in the 3rd, 4th, and 5th verses.

The rest of the chapter is dedicated to how a Yogi attains union at the time of his death, the way of release from the cycles of rebirth.

Krishna explains the cycles of Creation and Dissolution.

He explains how when one perfects self-control through constant Yogic discipline and awareness, all his life, He attains union and merges with supreme consciousness, at the time of death.

This chapter describes the material and spiritual dimensions of divine energies.

Deep introspection and contemplation is required for understanding creation in relation to the Self.

Cycles of cosmic creations and ways to get over the cycle of life and death are explained here.

This chapter deals with Knowing the absolute and understanding Creation in relation to the Spirit.

08

The Imperishable Absolute/Akshara Brahma Yoga

8.1-2

Arjuna uvāca:

kiṁ tad brahman kim adhyātmam kiṁ karma puruṣottama |
adhibhūtaṁ ca kiṁ proktam adhidaivaṁ kim ucyate ||

adhiyajñaḥ kathaṁ ko 'tra dehe 'smin madhusūdana |
prayāṇakāle ca kathaṁ jñeyo 'si niyatātmabhiḥ ||

Arjuna said:

O Best of the Purushas (Krishna)!

Please tell me, what is Brahman? What is Purushottam? What is Adhyatman?

What is Karma? What is Adhibhuta? And what is Adhidaiva?

O Slayer of the Demon Madhu (Krishna)! What is Adhiyajna? and in what manner is Adhiyajna present (as the soul) in this body? And how, at the time of death, art Thou to be known by the self-disciplined?

Explanation:

Q1. What is **Brahman**?

Ans: The Omniscient, Omnipresent and Omnipotent, the indestructible Spirit is Brahman. It is the field of unlimited potential and unlimited possibilities. It is the ultimate reality underlying all phenomenon. Refer to Chart 14.

Q2. What is **Adhyatman**?

Ans: *Adhyatman or Kutastha Chaitanya* is the undifferentiated manifestation of Brahman or that aspect that creates and causes manifestation of the Universe. It is the *Param atman* / Ishvara in causal world of the Macrocosm and *Pragya* in the causal body of the Microcosm. (the Kutastha Consciousness underlying all manifestations and existing as the soul of all beings in the cosmos)

Q3. What is *Karma*?

Ans: Aum is the Cosmic Vibration that causes the birth and sustenance and dissolution of beings and their various natures. This creation of the cosmos is termed as the karma [cosmic action] of Ishvara. (cosmic and meditative actions are born of Aum)

Q4. What is *Adhibhuta*? *Bhuta* (elements of matter)

Ans: *Adhibhuta* is the basis of the Physical world of the Macrocosm [*Virat*] and the physical body of the Microcosm [*Vishva*]. The consciousness immanent in physical creatures and the physical cosmos.

Q.5 What is *Adhidaiva*?

Ans: It is the basis of the Astral world. *Daiva* (*devas*) are Demi Gods. They are also the consciousness of Astral bodies and the Astral cosmos. The world or plane of heaven where Demi Gods play the role of Astral Angels or evolved souls, work in accordance and in alignment with the dictates of divinity. Astral world is that subtle space where Matter does not exist. (Where we rest after death of this body). The Devas are also created by Ishvara and assigned certain duties and *gunas*. Just as light passing thru A prism breaks up into myriad colors, but the source is one. When we pray to these Devas for the satisfaction of our desires, the prayers reach the Devas and desire satisfaction is achieved, but ultimately the source is Supreme Consciousness alone.

Adhidaiva is the basis of Astral /subtle world which we call heaven in the Macrocosm [Hiranyagarbha], and the basis of the Astral body in the microcosm [Tejas]. The consciousness manifests in astral bodies and the astral cosmos.

Q6. What is *Adhiyajna*?

Ans: *Adhiyajna* is *Ishvara* in the causal world *of* the Macrocosm and *Prajna* (highest form of intuition, wisdom and intelligence) in the causal body of the microcosm. It is the Spirit (*Purusha*) in us. It is Soul or *Atman*, the Supreme creative and cognizing Spirit.

Q7. How do we discipline ourselves at the time of **death?** Super question relevant for all of us.

Ans: Our thoughts at the last moments of life determine our next birth. In this verse it is very categorically, carefully and precisely stated that the "thought with which a dying man leaves the body determines his next state of being". Hence our Mind matter-the quality of our thoughts is our true wealth. We need to train and purify our thoughts by using our intellect and discrimination. We take our mind matter to our next life!

8.3

Srī Bhagavān uvāca:

akṣaraṁ brahma paramaṁ svabhāvo 'dhyātmam ucyate |
bhūtabhāvodbhavakaro visargaḥ karmasaṁjñitaḥ ||

The Blessed Supreme replied:
The Indestructible and Supreme Spirit is Brahman. Its undifferentiated manifestation (as Kutastha Chaitanya and as the individual soul) is called Adhyatman.

The Aum (Cosmic Vibration or the Visarga) that causes the birth and sustenance and dissolution of beings and their various natures is termed Karma (cosmic action).

Explanation:

Brahman	The Absolute, indestructible Supreme Spirit
Adhyatman	Brahman's undifferentiated Manifestation, as Ishvara in the macrocosm and Jivatma in the individual microcosm
Karma	Creative vibration - Cosmic action by Creation that causes manifestation

1. **Brahman** - The absolute, all-inclusive Spirit is that which exists beyond the vibratory **Aum**.

2. **Adhyatman is** the underlying Universal Soul or what we experience as the individual Soul.

3. **Cosmic Karma** is also the Karma of Ishvara. It is the Aum Vibration which creates Nature - *Mool Prakriti.* **Aum** is the cosmic vibration that manifests into sound and light resulting in Creation.

8.4

adhibhūtaṁ kṣaro bhāvaḥ puruṣaś cādhidaivatam |
adhiyajño 'ham evātra dehe dehabhṛtāṁ vara ||

O Supreme Among the Embodied (Arjuna)! Adhibhuta is the basis of physical existence, Adhidaiva is the basis of astral existence and I the Spirit within the body and the cosmos am Adhiyajna (the Causal Origin, the Great Sacrificer, the Maker and Cognizer of all)

Explanation:

Adhibhuta is the perishable physical existence. The presiding Deity governing the physical body of the cosmos or macrocosm is *Virat.* The presiding deity governing the physical body of the individual *Jiva atman* is *Vishva.*

Adhidaiva is the indweller, the faculty that presides over the apparatus and faculties of knowledge and activity of our subtle existence. The presiding Deity governing the astral body of the Cosmos is *Hiranyagarbha.* The presiding Deity governing the astral body of the individual *Jiva atman* is *Taijas.*

Adhiyajna is the Self, the principle of life, the Spirit. *Adhiyajna* is *Ishvara* the supreme spirit who creates the Cosmos, who is the Cause of Creation itself in the Macrocosm. He is called *Pragya or Prajna* in the causal body of the individual *Jiva atman.*

Adhi yagna	Universal spirit in the microcosm and the cosmos, the basis of Causal existence.
Adhi daiva	The basis of Astral existence.
Adhi bhuta	The basis of Physical existence.

Chart 16

Here we aim to inspire the understanding of the keen student, about the Macrocosm and the Microcosm. Man must remain unentangled in Maya and unencumbered by the delusion of the triple gunas.

	Microcosm = Kutastha Chaitanya + individual ego		Macrocosm = Kutastha Chaitanya + universal ego	
	Presiding Deities		**Presiding Deities**	
Causal Body	*Pragya*	*Adhiyagna*	*Ishvara*	**Causal World**
Subtle Body	*Taijas*	*Adhidaiva*	*Hiranyagharba*	**Subtle World**
Physical Body	*Vishwa*	*Adhibhuta*	*Virat*	**Physical world**

Chart 17

8.5

antakāle ca mām eva smaran muktvā kalevaram |
yaḥ prayāti sa madbhāvaṁ yāti nāsty atra saṁśayaḥ ||

Lastly, he enters My Being who thinks only of Me at the hour of his passing when the body is abandoned. This is truth beyond doubt.

Explanation:

Beyond any doubt our thoughts at the last moments of life determine our next birth.

As you can see in this verse it is very categorically, carefully and precisely stated that the "thought with which a dying man leaves the body determines his next state of being" describes what decides the destination of the soul after death. If we can visualize divinity at the time of departing from the body, we will certainly attain Him.

8.6

yaṁ yaṁ vāpi smaran bhāvaṁ tyajaty ante kalevaram |
taṁ tam evaiti kaunteya sadā tadbhāvabhāvitaḥ ||

O Son of Kunti (Arjuna), that thought with which a dying man leaves the body determines - through his long persistence in it - his next state of being.

Explanation:

Should we surrender the mind and the intellect? Yes, we should surrender to the intelligent cosmos with devotion. Most of us fear death, fear of the unknown. This is maybe because we doubt His Omnipresence.

Our next birth is determined by the persistence with which we carry our thoughts and desires, not only throughout our life but at the time of death. Investing in spirituality and living a life of spiritual awakening ensures that at the time of our passing away too, we will be absorbed in Him.

8.7

tasmāt sarveṣu kāleṣu mām anusmara yudhya ca |
mayy arpitamanobuddhir mām evaiṣyasy asaṁśayam ||

Therefore, remember Me always, and engage thyself in the battle of activity! Surrender to Me thy mind and thine understanding! Thus, without doubt shalt thou come unto Me.

Explanation:

Unless we constantly and habitually remember the divine source throughout our life and have surrendered to Him our very desires and our actions, it is not possible to be without fear and doubt at the time of death. A mind that is full of doubt cannot evolve but is caught in a dilemma of inaction. Such a mind is incapable of choice and is stagnant. A doubting mind cannot progress in any direction. Doubt, beyond curiosity, becomes a disease. Such a person will not find peace anywhere – not in this world, nor the next. Faith is loving the unknown-that which you have not experienced with your physical senses but with your intuition.

8.8

abhyāsayogayuktena cetasā nānyagāminā |
paramaṁ puruṣaṁ divyaṁ yāti pārthānucintayan ||

He attains the Supreme Effulgent Supreme, O Partha (Arjuna), whose mind, stabilized by yoga, is immovably fixed on the thought of Him.

Explanation:

Our body, it's daily drama of activity, the mind with its sensory impressions and the discriminative intellect gets emotionally agitated. We can stabilize the self by withdrawing our senses from the outside world through *Pratyahara*, and the *Pranayama* techniques help to divert the life current of the 5 senses from external stimuli to internal stability and still its restless fluctuations. These fluctuations are nothing but thoughts that keep appearing in our mind. With constant practice of Pranayama, these fluctuations can be minimized and focus on the Real Self improved. Meditation helps a Yogi to focus on the very core of existence, the very source, and helps in kindling true awareness. This awareness is the mother of all wisdom.

8.9-10

kaviṁ purāṇam anuśāsitāram aṇor aṇīyāṁsam anusmared yaḥ |
sarvasya dhātāram acintyarūpam ādityavarṇaṁ tamasaḥ parastāt ||

prayāṇakāle manasācalena bhaktyā yukto yogabalena caiva |
bhruvor madhye prāṇam āveśya samyak sa taṁ paraṁ puruṣam
upaiti divyam ||

At the time of death a yogi reaches the effulgent Supreme, if with love and by the power of yoga, he fully penetrates his life.

force between the eyebrows (the seat of the spiritual eye), and if he fixes his mind unwaveringly on the Being who, beyond all.

delusions of darkness, shines like the sun-the One whose form is.

unimaginable, subtler than the finest atom, the Supporter of all, the Great Ruler, eternal and omniscient.

<u>Explanation:</u>

This verse is a great lesson on "death" and how to prepare for the inevitable changing of body. Mostly we are unprepared for death, and our ego enters a tug of war with death as desire of this physical life remains strong.

Regular practice of Yogic techniques helps to stabilize the wavering Mind. Sincere, persistent practice and total love and surrender is required. The technique described here of focusing our life energies between the eyebrows, the seat of the spiritual eye or *Agya chakra*, is used by advanced Yogis to meditate on the omniscient, all powerful, most effulgent Divinity. When done regularly, It requires no effort at the time of death.

These are the 3 qualifications to merge into Divine essence:

Love of the Divine and Creation (Knowing Thy Self)
Mastery of Raja / Kriya Yoga science
Perfect Control of the Mind.

8.11

yad akṣaraṁ vedavido vadanti viśanti yad yatayo vītarāgāḥ |
yad icchanto brahmacaryaṁ caranti tat te padaṁ saṁgraheṇa pravakṣye ||

That which the Vedic seers declare as the Immutable, That which is gained by renunciants of vanished attachments, desiring which, they lead a life of self-discipline-the method for attaining. That I will relate to thee in brief.

<u>Explanation:</u>

What is to be attained? How do we attain the Brahman? This verse indicates how one can progress on the path of spiritual evolvement. We have to carefully avoid attachment to the external enticements by adopting a life of restraint and cultivating self-discipline diligently. By practicing the <u>eight-fold path of yoga,</u> the self-discipline required can be cultivated.

Patanjali's Eight-fold ashtanga yoga path explained: Yama, Niyama, Asanas, Pranayama, Pratyahara, Dharana, Dhyana, Samadhi.

1. YAMAS	RESPECT FOR OTHERS
2. NIYAMAS	RESPECT FOR YOURSELF
3. ASANAS	HARMONY WITH YOUR BODY
4. PRANAYAMA	HARMONY WITH YOUR ENERGY
5. PRATYAHARA	HARMONY WITH YOUR EMOTIONS
6. DHARANA	HARMONY WITH YOUR THOUGHTS
7. DHYANA	CONTEMPLATION
8. SAMADHI	BLISS & ECSTASY

Chart 18

8.12-13

sarvadvārāṇi saṁyamya mano hṛdi nirudhya ca
mūrdhny ādhāyātmanaḥ prāṇam āsthito yogadhāraṇām
om ity ekākṣaraṁ brahma vyāharan mām anusmaran
yaḥ prayāti tyajan dehaṁ sa yāti paramāṁ gatim

He who closes the nine gates of the body, who cloisters the mind in the heart center, who fixes the full life force in the cerebrum- he who thus engages in the steady practice of yoga, establishing himself in

Aum, the Holy Word of Brahman, and remembering Me (Spirit) at the time of his final exit from the body, reaches the highest Goal.

Explanation:

In this verse a vital technique of Kriya Yoga (Raja Yoga) is explained. Each sense organ is an aperture in the body drawing our attention to the external world. We need to shut these doors through discrimination and detachment. We have to have a mind that is qualified to know we are ignorant. Only then the pursuit of true knowledge can be embarked upon. A conscious effort is required to grow in the path of spirituality.

What are the 9 Gates of the body?

2 x Eyes	To see, observe
2 x Nostrils	To smell
2 x Ears	To hear
Mouth	To taste and talk
Genitalia	To procreate
Anus	To eliminate

Chart 19

Here three kinds of meditation are presented:

Meditating on the Universal Cosmic form
Meditating on the Cosmic Sound AUM
Chanting the name of Ishvara constantly

Chart 20

8.14

ananyacetāḥ satataṁ yo māṁ smarati nityaśaḥ |
tasyāhaṁ sulabhaḥ pārtha nityayuktasya yoginaḥ ||

O Partha (Arjuna)! I am easily reached by that yogi who is singlehearted,
who remembers Me daily, continually, his mind intensely focused only on Me.

Explanation:

Deep focus and concentration are required to keep the mind on the one Goal.... Realisation.

This world is a finishing school. The highest lesson here is the realisation that we are not mortal but free and liberated children of Mother Earth. Bhakti Yoga, the path of devotion is considered better and easier than *Jnana Yoga* [the path of knowledge] and *Karma Yoga* [the path of Selfless action]. As both without devotion are incomplete. We need to choose one path and follow diligently.

8.15

mām upetya punarjanma duḥkhālayam aśāśvatam |
nāpnuvanti mahātmānaḥ saṁsiddhiṁ paramāṁ gatāḥ ||

My noble devotees, having obtained Me (Spirit), have reached.
supreme success: they incur no further rebirths in this abode of
grief **and transitoriness.**

Explanation:

Reaching the success of non-separateness the yogi incurs no rebirth as there remains no karmic baggage. When the final union is achieved there is no rebirth. When True awareness and brilliance come to the yogi, the fire of knowledge burns the seeds of Karma. Through Yoga he becomes centered and lets go of the feverishness of desire and renounces the fruit of action. He maintains stability of the intellect by commitment. He then rises above the law of karma and is free.

8.16

ā brahmabhuvanāl lokāḥ punarāvartino 'rjuna |
mām upetya tu kaunteya punarjanma na vidyate ||

Yogis not yet free from the world revolve back again (to the world) even from the high sphere of Brahma (union with Brahman in samadhi). But on entering Me (the transcendental Spirit) there is no rebirth, O son of Kunti (Arjuna)!

Explanation:

Even from the highest state of *Samadhi* (when consciousness has merged with the primordial vibratory OM) we can revolve back into body consciousness of the *Karan Sharira* (Causal Body) which is persistent with desires and karmic bondages.

The inhabitants of the world are subject to the finite law of recurrence (rebirth into finite body) Man can only escape this law if he comes into "himself" or in other words merges into the absolute (*shoonya*).

Yogis keep coming back even from the highest realm of spiritual ecstasy or *Samadhi*, if they have not completely conquered their mind.

8.17-19

sahasrayugaparyantam ahar yad brahmaṇo viduḥ
rātriṁ yugasahasrāntāṁ te 'horātravido janāḥ ||

avyaktād vyaktayaḥ sarvāḥ prabhavanty aharāgame |
rātryāgame pralīyante tatraivāvyaktasaṁjñake ||

bhūtagrāmaḥ sa evāyaṁ bhūtvā bhūtvā pralīyate |
rātryāgame 'vaśaḥ pārtha prabhavaty aharāgame ||

They are true knowers of "day" and "night" who understands the Day of Brahma, which endures for a thousand cycles (yugas), and the Night of Brahma, which also endures for a thousand cycles.

At the dawn of Brahma's Day all creation, reborn, emerges from the state of non-manifestation; at the dusk of Brahma's Night all creation sinks into the sleep of non-manifestation.

Again and again, O son of Pritha (Arjuna), the same throng of men helplessly take rebirth. Their series of incarnations ceases at the coming of Night, and then reappears at the dawn of Day.

Explanation:

Day (1000 cycles) and Night of Brahma (1000 cycles)

Incarnations appear at the Dawn of Brahma's Day

Incarnations stop at the coming of Night. Except for a few liberated men, the same multitude of beings are reborn many times during a day of Brahma. They rest [without further reincarnations] during the night of cosmic Dissolution. When the cycle of creation restarts, again they start the karmically compulsory journeys! However as per Parmahansa Yogananda's teaching (8.23-26) if a human dies when he is in personal spiritual ascent into knowledge or descent into sensory world that then determines his next birth.

Many astrologers and ancient gurus taught that these verses determined where the soul would rest according to time and season of death.

One Yuga Cycle = 24000 Human / Solar Years

Ascending Cycle = 12000 human years

Satya Yuga	4800 Years	Spiritual Age
Treta Yuga	3600 Years	Mental Age
Dvapar Yuga	2400 Years	Atomic Age
Kali Yuga	1200 Years	Material Age

Chart 21 A

Descending cycle. = 12000 human years

Kali Yuga	1200 Years	Material Age
Dvapar Yuga	2400 Years	Atomic Age
Treta Yuga	3600 Years	Mental Age
Satya Yuga	4800 Years	Spiritual Age

Chart 21 B

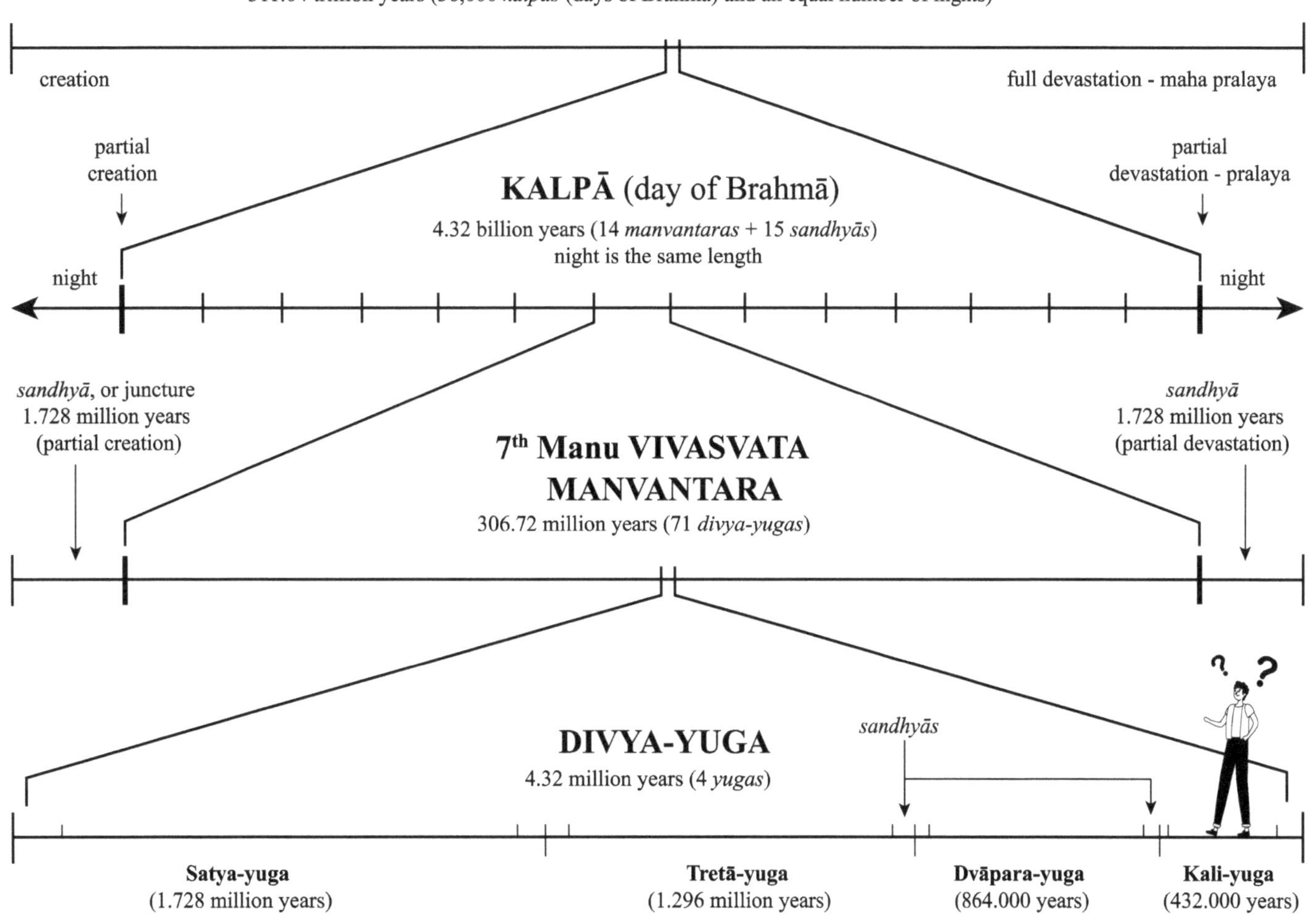

8.20

paras tasmāt tu bhāvo 'nyo 'vyakto 'vyaktāt sanātanaḥ |
yaḥ sa sarveṣu bhūteṣu naśyatsu na vinaśyati ||

But transcending the unmanifested (states of phenomenal being) there exists the true Unmanifested, the Immutable, the Absolute, which remains untouched by the cycles of cosmic dissolution.

Explanation:

The comings and goings of the Universe start from Brahma, but this is also transitory as even Brahma the creator has a span of existence lasting of 100 Divine years, after which another Brahma is created. But beyond the triune of Brahma, Vishnu, Mahesh, and beyond the cycles of Time and Space, is the indestructible, unchangeable, un manifested, ever-lasting substratum - Brahman.

As time is not linear in the eternal consciousness, this entire creation is but one moment. Man's birth is all emotional. We respond to stimuli that we identify as pleasurable or disagreeable according to our individual likes *(Raga)* and dislikes *(Dvesha)*.

This Moha (attachment) and game of sense pleasures is a delusion, as the body is a temporary object subjected to Maya.

Sat	Brahman	The absolute Truth. Is nonexistence and existence itself. Eternal and infinite. Untouched by any cycle. The Ultimate Source or Supreme Source.
Tat or Ishvara	As Brahma	It is the undifferentiated and unmanifested reflection of Brahman's Creative Consciousness
	As Vishnu	as the Preserver holds the seed form in the night of dissolution and the day of projection or involution
	As Shiva	Manifestation and Dissolution
Om	The holy Ghost	Creative Vibration that manifests

Chart 22

Rig Veda Mandala 10 Sukta 129

1. "Then was not nonexistent nor existent there was no realm of air, no sky beyond it.
What covered in, and where? and what gave shelter? Was water there, unfathomed depth of water?

2. Death was not then, nor was there aught immortal: no sign was there, the day's and night's divider.
That One Thing, breathless, breathed by its own nature: apart from it was nothing whatsoever.

3. Darkness there was: at first concealed in darkness this All was indiscriminate chaos.
All that existed then was void and form less: by the great power of Warmth was born that Unit.

4. Thereafter rose Desire in the beginning, Desire, the primal seed and germ of Spirit.
Sages who searched with their heart's thought discovered the existent's kinship in the non-existent.

5. Transversely was their severing line extended: what was above it then, and what below it? There were begetters, there were mighty forces, free action here and energy up yonder

6. Who verily knows and who can here declare it, whence it was born and whence comes this creation?
The Gods are later than this world's production. Who knows then whence it first came into being?

7. He, the first origin of this creation, whether he formed it all or did not form it, Whose eye controls this world in highest heaven, he verily knows it, or perhaps he knows not.

8.21-22

avyakto 'kṣara ity uktas tam āhuḥ paramāṁ gatim |
yaṁ prāpya na nivartante tad dhāma paramaṁ mama ||

puruṣaḥ sa paraḥ pārtha bhaktyā labhyas tv ananyayā |
yasyāntaḥsthāni bhūtāni yena sarvam idaṁ tatam ||

The aforesaid Unmanifested, the Immutable Absolute, is thus called the Supreme Goal. Those who attain it, My highest state, undergo no more rebirth.

By singlehearted devotion, O son of Pritha (Arjuna), that Supreme Unmanifested is reached. He alone, the Omnipresent, is the Abode of all creatures.

Explanation:

Once attaining the absolute there is no more "rebirth". Only through single one-pointed devotion is the absolute reached.

8.23-26

yatra kāle tv anāvṛttim āvṛttiṁ caiva yoginaḥ |
prayātā yānti taṁ kālaṁ vakṣyāmi bharatarṣabha ||

agnir jyotir ahaḥ śuklaḥ ṣaṇmāsā uttarāyaṇam |
tatra prayātā gacchanti brahma brahmavido janāḥ ||

dhūmo rātris tathā kṛṣṇaḥ ṣaṇmāsā dakṣiṇāyanam |
tatra cāndramasaṁ jyotir yogī prāpya nivartate ||

śuklakṛṣṇe gatī hy ete jagataḥ śāśvate mate |
ekayā yāty anāvṛttim anyayāvartate punaḥ ||

I shall now declare unto thee, O Best of the Bharatas (Arjuna), the path, traversing which at the time of death, yogis attain freedom; and the path wherein there is rebirth.

Fire, light, daytime, the bright half of the lunar month, the six months of the northern course of the sun, pursuing this path at the time of departure, the knowers of Brahman go to Brahman.

Smoke, nighttime, the dark half of the lunar month, the six months of the southern course of the sun, he who follows this path obtains only the lunar light and then returns to earth.

These two paths for exiting from the world are reckoned eternal. The way of light leads to release, the way of darkness leads to rebirth.

The two paths of exiting this world:

That of light	That of darkness
Leads to moksha / release	Leads to rebirth
Fire	Smoke
Bright half of lunar month	Dark half of the lunar month
6 months of northern course of sun	6 months of southern course of the sun

<u>Chart 23</u>

<u>Explanation:</u>

In 8.23-26 Krishna says, "I will declare the path traversing which at the time of death there will be no return".

If we pass away in the summer months of April to October, between sunrise to midday, in the days when the moon is waxing increasing - *Amavasya* (no moon) to Full moon, it is an ascent and auspicious cycle.

The descent cycle is the opposite when sun is setting, moon is waning (decreasing) and the months are in winter, this person must be reborn again to balance his karma".

The verse above, very clearly states that we ought to be in the evolving path of knowledge and light to be released from the darkness and delusion of next birth.

If one learns to focus on the Divine now, then at the time of death naturally, one will think of nothing else. Or else, in the chaos of death, one would probably panic and lose their way.

The path of renunciation can be followed internally and externally. Outer renunciation is superficial and not as beneficial as destroying internal desires & attachments from sense temptations.

8.27-28

> naite sṛtī pārtha jānan yogī muhyati kaścana |
> tasmāt sarveṣu kāleṣu yogayukto bhavārjuna (27) ||
>
> vedeṣū yajñeṣu tapaḥsu caiva dāneṣu yat puṇyaphalaṁ pradiṣṭam |
> atyeti tat sarvam idaṁ viditvā yogī paraṁ sthānam upaiti cādyam || (28)

No yogi who understands these two paths is ever deluded (into following the way of darkness). Therefore, O Arjuna! Always maintain thyself firmly in yoga.

He who knows the truth about the two paths gains merit far beyond any implicit in the study of the scriptures, or in sacrifices, or in penances, or in gift-giving. That yogi reaches his Supreme Origin (Source).

Explanation:

This is the time to introduce "Me" - Me as in Brahman the Creator; the Source or Me as the Self. Eventually in spirituality both the "ME" and the "Me" becomes one - That Union is called YOG. In this union the small I self, disappears into the Big I (Brahman)

What are these two paths that have been elaborated in this verse?

1. Path towards darkness, ignorance and towards sensory world, getting more and more attached and karmically bound (descent)

2. Path towards the spiritual light of knowledge, going toward self-realisation (ascent)

Task 3: What is the connotation associated by the terms path of darkness and path of light as per Vēdānta?

Summary of Chapter 8

The Imperishable Absolute/ Akshara Brahma Yoga

In this chapter, Krishna gives us a deeper understanding of the working of the universe and how to attain freedom from the cycle of rebirth, through pure understanding and knowledge (*Jnana*).

The manifestation of spirit in the Macrocosm and Microcosm as *Adhiyagna* in the causal world and the causal body; as *Adhidaiva* in the astral world and the astral body; and as *Adhibhuta* in the physical world and physical body is described in the first few verses.

Constitution of physical cosmic nature or matter is thoughtrons of God, lifetrons, electrons, protons, atoms, molecules, cells, tissue and organic matter. Both Organic and Inorganic matter are composed of Anu, Paramanu, Prana and Chaitanya [Consciousness]

The Self is the reality upon which all actions, the instruments of action, and the world of perceptions are super-imposed and therefore when the Self is known, All is known.

Our Solar System moves around a magnetic center in the cosmos, in a 24000 –year cycle, referred to as the equinoctial cycle consisting of four yugas [Kali, Dvapara, Treta and Satya], in a 12000 ascending arc and 12000 descending arcs.

Similarly, man's individual evolution is marked by the cycles of his miniature solar cosmos- the energizing effect of the spiritual eye on the astral centers of the spine.

With focused work on the Astral Centers [The Chakras], along the spine, The Yogi is able to evolve spiritually.

The sincere kriya yogi may achieve liberation in 3, 6, 12, 24 or 48 years, or a few additional incarnations.

The practical aspect and techniques of attaining Self-Realisation are described in the rest of the chapter.

Accepting the human ability of free will we need to utilize this birth for attaining moksha. Being in this body is necessary to achieve Moksha as we have the Intellect as equipment given to us to develop discrimination in order to make the choice. Spiritual evolution is a choice each Jiva atman has to make.

Sages know how to do this and try to balance their karma in this one lifetime, so they don't remain in the cycle of birth and death for too long.

Praying to the *Devas* for bestowing gifts upon us without undertaking the knowledge and action path will play no purpose in the eventual evolvement of our individual soul.

Vēdānta and all the scriptures have within them the knowledge that Man' is seeking. Yogi's and Sages, who have studied and practiced Raja Yoga and those who have been born with incomplete spiritual journeys continue this path, clinging to the one desire of "Knowing the Self".

The highest state of realisation is freedom from the bodily, sensory, and worldly consciousness.

Once attaining the absolute there is no more "Rebirth" Only through single one-pointed devotion is the absolute reached.

Believing in a finite form of an infinite, Omnipotent, Omniscient and Omnipresent source, is unwise. We worship various forms, but these forms do not hold within them the complete ideal possibilities that is <u>Ishvara or Aham Brahmasmi.</u>

For example, the great sage, Rama Krishna Paramhansa worshipped the Goddess Kali, but he had to destroy the finite form of Mother Kali with the sword of wisdom just so he could behold her as the formless infinite Brahman.

<u>Task 4: Name all the aspects of the eight-fold yoga system</u>

<u>Task 5: Prepare a chart of the chronological cycle of the universe / Yugas - life of Brahma etc. as per these verses.</u>

Om   Creative Vibration

Tat   Ishvara or Kutastha Chaitanya

Sat   Brahman

Comments by nascent seekers of Vēdānta studies:

It is interesting to inspire the understanding of the keen student about the Macrocosm and the Microcosm.

Man must remain unentangled in Maya and unencumbered by the delusion of the triple Gunas - Satva Rajas Tamas.

Satva Rajas Tamas are the triple modes of Nature and are the operating principles or tendencies of all beings.

The Gunas are a magnificent lesson in themselves.

It's a hypnotic world out there. Life and its experience are entertainment. Observe the unfolding of life as a witness without attachment.

Maya itself is an interplay of Satva: Goodness, purity. Rajas: Passion, activity, and Tamas: imbalanced ignorance and inertia.

The Spirit is not affected at any time, whilst we, the ego self gets caught up through the influence of gunas and is lost in this world and its gameplay.

Instead of seeking his gifts, seek the answers of Creation and pursue knowledge.

He who aligns with the vibration of the universe is the favorite of the Lord.

The seeker of the Self attains union with the divine.

Every day we wake up and then we die (sleep), and we live an average of 27,000 days and 27,000 nights in 75 years. Each day and each night are a chance for us to transcend one Birth.

Sages know how to perform Raja Yoga and try to balance their karma in this one lifetime, so they don't remain in the cycle of birth and death for too long.

Karma Yoga - Is doing the right action with non-doer ship / non ego / not focused on the fruit of action / nonattachment.

Karma Yoga also includes in its domain, doing the important right action of withdrawing the mind from the senses. This feat is the ultimate **Karma.** In this *tapasya* the life force energy is centered between the eyebrows and our mind is united with the wisdom of the Soul.

BHAGAVAD GITA VOLUME – 2

Chapter 9

The Royal knowledge, the Royal mystery - *Raja vidya Raja guhiya yoga*

Introduction to Chapter 9

In this chapter, the discussion is not only of the theory of self-perfection, but also of the logic behind it all. Vēdānta is not a religion; it provides a scientific explanation for the universal way of right living.

Here Krishna puts forth an easily understandable, easily comprehensible science pertaining to a life lived with awareness of what is right and what is wrong, and the science of The Self, the deepest essence in everyone.

It is not blind faith and practice of rituals, but *shraddha* which is the faith and devotion born of personal experience and intuition, that is extolled here.

This is an exciting chapter where an esoteric spiritual secret is revealed

What secret? The secret of intuitive knowledge to achieve union of individual Spirit with the Universal Spirit – Yog or Yuj, is revealed here.

With focused work on the Astral Centers [The Chakras], along the spine, The Yogi can evolve spiritually.

Through Meditation and one-pointed devotion, one can transcend the cosmic cycle of birth and death and become one with the creator.

Union with the absolute Spirit happens when we became one with Him. This is known as Self-Realisation, Yoga or Advait.

The relationship between the Absolute and His creation, [The lower Nature] is explained.

The practical aspect and techniques of attaining Self - Realisation are described in this chapter. Through constant Yogic practices, Meditation, and constant contemplation on the Absolute Spirit, one can attain Moksha.

Our only Dharma is "Self-Realisation". The only purpose of being born as a human being with intellect and power of discrimination is to seek this True knowledge. This highest truth can only be known by the experience of life in this earthly form and making the choice of becoming a seeker.

The Royal knowledge, the Royal mystery - *Raja vidya Raja guhiya yoga*

9.1-3

Srī Bhagavān uvāca:

idaṁ tu te guhyatamaṁ pravakṣyāmy anasūyave |
jñānaṁ vijñānasahitaṁ yaj jñātvā mokṣyase 'śubhāt (1) ||

rājavidyā rājaguhyaṁ pavitram idam uttamam |
pratyakṣāvagamaṁ dharmyaṁ susukhaṁ kartum avyayam (2) ||

aśraddadhānāḥ puruṣā dharmasyāsya paraṁtapa |
aprāpya māṁ nivartante mṛtyusaṁsāravartmani (3) ||

The Blessed Supreme said:

To thee, the uncarping one, I shall now reveal the sublime mystery (the immanent-transcendent nature of Spirit) of Nirguna Brahman [unmanifest Divinity]; and Sagun Brahman [manifest divinity]. Possessing intuitive Realisation of this wisdom, thou shalt escape from evil of worldly existence.

This intuitive Realisation is the king of sciences, the royal secret, the peerless purifier, the essence of dharma (man's righteous duty); it is the direct perception of truth-the imperishable enlightenment-attained through the ways of yoga which are very easy to perform.

Men without faith in this dharma (without devotion to the practices that bestow Realisation) attain Me not, O Scorcher of Foes (Arjuna)! Again and again, they tread the death darkened path of samsara (the rounds of rebirth).

<u>Explanation:</u>

Uncarping? To have an open mind, uncritical and without doubt, in deep faith. We have to be in an acceptance mode. When purified from all the above, we become ready to imbibe this knowledge that is about to be revealed. Intense devotion and perseverance is needed in order to achieve this union.

The intuitive knowledge that comes to us through energizing of the *Agya* (*Ajna*) chakra is the Royal Secret of the Raja Rishi's.

It is the experience of this doorway to knowledge, the 1000 petalled lotus, which illuminates within us during deep meditation. Perfect intuition and Jnana- the illumination of the Jiva atman happens.

Men who do not perceive this realisation of the Self, and do not seek this, will forever remain trapped in the earthly cycle of death and rebirth.

Sri Krishna explains in this verse that Brahman, the Supreme Consciousness, is formless and Nirguna [without the 3 gunas that qualify prakriti or the manifested universe] before he begins to manifest the universe. He is Saguna as well, when He is Kutastha Chaitanya-Ishvara causing manifestation of the universe. As Saguna Brahman he can take form and appear as an Avatar.

9.4-6

mayā tatam idaṁ sarvaṁ jagad avyaktamūrtinā |
matsthāni sarvabhūtāni na cāhaṁ teṣv avasthitaḥ (4) ||

na ca matsthāni bhūtāni paśya me yogam aiśvaram |
bhūtabhṛn na ca bhūtastho mamātmā bhūtabhāvanaḥ ||

yathākāśasthito nityaṁ vāyuḥ sarvatrago mahān |
tathā sarvāṇi bhūtāni matsthānīty upadhāraya ||

I, the Unmanifested, pervade the whole universe. All creatures abide in Me, but I do not abide in them.

Behold My Divine Mystery! in which all beings are apparently not in Me, nor does My Self dwell in them; yet I alone am them.

Creator and Preserver!

Understand it thus: Just as air moves freely in the infinitudes of space (akasha) and has its being in space (yet air is different from space), just so do all creatures have their being in Me (but they are not I).

<u>Explanation:</u>

"Creatures abide in me" but "I do not abide in them". So how come "Aham Brahmasmi"?

The whole of the universe is permeated by the unmanifested Brahman. Although He creates and sustains the universe, he does not depend on it nor is involved in it.

Brahman is not the individual soul (*Jiva Atman*) He is the Universal Soul (Param *Atman*). Yet He pervades every being. Human reason cannot grasp the meaning of creation, only intuition can resolve it.

All that is precious in life is a secret. Existence itself is a big secret. Our limited intellect and logic cannot fathom it. So, honor the secret, accept it. Then the mind stabilizes and starts to blossom! Honoring the secret is *Shradha* (devotion), it is keeping the mind open to what is beyond our knowing mind and adoring it.

All the contradictions in verses 4-5 only appears as an illusion. The discriminating buddhi / intellect can at once dissolve all the shadow and come into light.

The Supreme Consciousness is in all beings, and everything is in Him – He is all pervasive yet remains transcendent. He created the universe but does not get involved in it nor is he affected by it. He exists in our Soul, creating and supporting us, yet He, himself does not get entangled in us.

9.7-8

> sarvabhūtāni kaunteya prakṛtiṁ yānti māmikām |
> kalpakṣaye punas tāni kalpādau visṛjāmy aham ||
>
> prakṛtiṁ svām avaṣṭabhya visṛjāmi punaḥ punaḥ |
> bhūtagrāmam imaṁ kṛtsnam avaśaṁ prakṛter vaśāt ||

At the end of a cycle (kalpa), O Son of Kunti (Arjuna), all beings return to the unmanifested state of My Cosmic Nature (Prakriti). At the beginning of the next cycle, again I cast them forth.

By re vivifying Prakriti, Mine own emanation, again and again I produce this host of creatures; all subject to the finite laws of Nature.

<u>Explanation:</u>

The Cycle of evolution - Kalpas - Yugas are sometimes Ascending and sometimes Descending.

The Om / vibration /energy re vivifies Prakriti and all creatures come forth. They are subject to the incontrovertible laws of Prakriti, causing Creation, Sustenance and Dissolution, which is cyclic. *Srishti and Pralay* occur in seemingly unending cycles.

Except for a few liberated men, the same multitude of beings are reborn many times during a day of Brahma. They rest [without further reincarnations] during the night of cosmic Dissolution. When the cycle of creation restarts, again they start the karmically compulsory journeys!

9.9

na ca māṁ tāni karmāṇi nibadhnanti dhanaṁjaya |
udāsīnavad āsīnam asaktaṁ teṣu karmasu ||

**But these activities entrammel Me not, O Winner of Wealth (Arjuna),
for I remain above them, aloof and unattached.**

Explanation:

The karmic pattern of action and inaction do not bind me as I remain an unattached witness to my own creation! I remain uninvolved even though I am emanant in everything!

Karmic bindings are created by man himself through attachment, misuse, and good use of free will choice. Attachment, desires and cravings cause the mind to be agitated. When the mind has no cravings, then there is Freedom.

9.10

mayādhyakṣeṇa prakṛtiḥ sūyate sacarācaram |
hetunānena kaunteya jagad viparivartate ||

**O Son of Kunti (Arjuna), it is solely My impregnating presence that
causes Mother Nature to give birth to the animate and the inanimate.
Because of Me (through Prakriti) the worlds revolve in alternating
cycles (of creation and dissolution).**

Explanation:

Brahman is the hidden essence of all manifestation. Nature with her infinite variety and inexorable laws is an evolute of the singular reality through cosmic delusion or Maya. The cycles of Creation and Dissolution of the universes are the *Maya* of Brahman alone. Both *Chara* [mobile - animate] and *Achara* [immobile or inanimate] are part of the manifested *Prakriti*.

Consciousness pervades the whole universe in various degrees:

Earth has	1 unit of consciousness
Water has	2 units of consciousness
Fire has	3 units of consciousness
Air has	4 units of consciousness
Space has	5 units of consciousness
Trees have	6 units of consciousness
Animals have	7 units of consciousness
Humans have	8 units of consciousness
Siddhas have	9 units of consciousness

Chart 24

Humans have the potential to develop 16 units of life [extraordinary human beings]

If we see Brahman as a field of unlimited potential, we shall see that the *maya* created by him is to experience human potential in a field of unlimited possibility! The separation between the Creator and his creation is only apparent!

9.11-12

avajānanti māṁ mūḍhā mānuṣīṁ tanum āśritam |
paraṁ bhāvam ajānanto mama bhūtamaheśvaram ||

moghāśā moghakarmāṇo moghajñānā vicetasaḥ |
rākṣasīm āsurīṁ caiva prakṛtiṁ mohinīṁ śritāḥ |

The ignorant, oblivious of My transcendental nature as the Maker of all creatures, discount also My presence within the human form.

Lacking in insight, their desires and thoughts and actions all vain, such men possess the deluded nature of fiends and demons.

<u>Explanation:</u>

Ignorance is this oblivion, the not knowingness, the delusion of being unaware of the Supreme Spirit. Those who live in complete disregard of the Spirit, are guided by their senses and are slaves to their desires, their Likes and Dislikes (raga dvesha). They are unaware of the real prowess of the Creator who can take any form when he wishes to and appear as an *Avatar* in this world too.

They live a life of delusion, of sense gratification, of finite pleasures. They must necessarily return to the path of rebirth, fraught with death.

9.13-15

> mahātmānas tu māṁ pārtha daivīṁ prakṛtim āśritāḥ |
> bhajanty ananyamanaso jñātvā bhūtādim avyayam ||
>
> satataṁ kīrtayanto māṁ yatantaś ca dṛḍhavratāḥ |
> namasyantaś ca māṁ bhaktyā nityayuktā upāsate ||
>
> jñānayajñena cāpy anye yajanto mām upāsate |
> ekatvena pṛthaktvena bahudhā viśvatomukham ||

But mahatma's ("great souls"), O Son of Pritha (Arjuna), expressing in their nature divine qualities, offer the homage of their undeviating minds to Me, knowing Me as the imperishable Source of all life.

Constantly absorbed in Me, bowing low with adoration, fixed and resolute in their high aspiration, they worship Me and ever. praise My name.

Others, also, performing the yajna of knowledge, worship Me, the Cosmic-Bodied Supreme, in various ways-first as the Many, and then as the One.

<u>Explanation:</u>

"Surrender of the self to the self" - this is of utmost importance - drop doer ship and ego of the small self and recognize that it is always the Self (Paramatman), that is the doer. Surrender to the Creator's master plan of the universe. Be the medium through which the universe operates in perfection.

Jnana is the path, the only path. The essence of worship is to know what is to be known, what is that which is to be known? The Supreme Self by the self, ultimate worship is this secret.

The lesson here is something even more magical and special. self-realisation is indeed self-realisation of one's own power potencies and potential to become one with the universe. Union with the absolute spirit happens when Him and us became one—Self-Realisation—realizing the divinity within us. We then live our lives as his extensions.

Those who do not have this realisation are not centered. They live with their eyes shut [e.g. Dhritrashtra] and when they die, they are in a joyless state.

Our journey is from *Dvait to Advait*; from worshipping Brahman in various forms (*Sakar*), to worshipping him as *Nirakaar Brahman,* the supreme Self, not separate from the Self.

9.16

ahaṁ kratur ahaṁ yajñaḥ svadhāhaṁ aham auṣadham |
mantro 'ham aham evājyam aham agnir ahaṁ hutam ||

I am the rite, the sacrifice, the oblation to ancestors, the medicinal herb, the holy chant, the melted butter, the sacred fire, and the offering.

Explanation:

Brahman is the essence behind all actions. Ritualistic actions constitute worship. All methods of worship – the rituals prescribed by the Vedas, the Yagnas, are nothing but worship of the Spirit. Here the action and the purpose of action in the form of worship also become One.

Just as a mass of gold is in a necklace, a ring or a pendant, so is the same Consciousness pervading every form of Creation.

9.17

pitāham asya jagato mātā dhātā pitāmahaḥ |
vedyaṁ pavitram oṁkāra ṛk sāma yajur eva ca ||

Of this world I am the father, the mother, the Ancestor, the Preserver, the Sanctifier, the all-inclusive Object of Knowledge, the Cosmic Aum, and the Vedic lore.

Explanation:

The finite relationships of the world are mentioned to depict the pure love that the blissful Self is. This Self is the substratum of the whole world, the entire universe, symbolized by Omkara. OM It is the only Knowledge worth knowing. Once Known, all else becomes Trivial!

9.18

gatir bhartā prabhuḥ sākṣī nivāsaḥ śaraṇaṁ suhṛt |
prabhavaḥ pralayaḥ sthānaṁ nidhānaṁ bījam avyayam ||

I am the Ultimate Goal, the Upholder, the Master, the Witness, the Shelter, the Refuge, and the One Friend. I am the Origin, the Dissolution, the Foundation, the Cosmic Storehouse, and the Seed Indestructible

Explanation:

Because I am the Atman of all beings, coming to me is recognizing Oneself. When we gain ourselves in terms of knowledge, we come to Ishvara. Brahman is reaching the Self. When we are free of delusion, Self-Realisation dawns, we realize that the Substratum for the whole diversity of existence is actually only One - The Cosmic Consciousness!

9.19

tapāmy aham ahaṁ varṣaṁ nigṛhṇāmy utsṛjāmi ca |
amṛtaṁ caiva mṛtyuś ca sad asac cāham Arjuna ||

I bestow solar heat, O Arjuna, and give or withhold the rain. Immortality am I, and Death; I am Being (Sat) and Non-Being (Asat).

Explanation:

Innate qualities explained. An average man is very serious about the worldly spectacle, a Yogi is only serious about knowing Brahman, the Self. Operating out of the *satvik, rajasik* and *tamasik* qualities (*gunas*) of nature the entire play of the world is of light and shadow, knowledge and ignorance, illumination and darkness, truth and delusion.

9.20-21

traividyā māṁ somapāḥ pūtapāpā yajñair iṣṭvā svargatiṁ Prārthayante |
te puṇyam āsādya surendralokam aśnanti divyān divi devabhogān (20) ||

te taṁ bhuktvā svargalokaṁ viśālaṁ kṣīṇe puṇye martyalokaṁ Viśanti |
evaṁ trayīdharmam anuprapannā gatāgataṁ kāmakāmā labhante ||

The Veda ritualists, cleansing themselves of sin by the soma rite, worship Me by yajna (sacrifice), and thus win their desire of entry into heaven.

There, in the sacred kingdom of the astral deities, devotees enjoy the subtle celestial pleasures.

But after delighting in the glorious higher regions, such. beings, at the expiration of their good karma, return to earth. Thus, abiding by the scriptural regulations, desiring the enjoyments (the promised celestial rewards thereof), they travel the cyclic path. (between heaven and earth).

Explanation:

"The small pleasures on the earthly plane I shall grant you through rituals, pooja's, *havan's, homas* and other vedic fire ceremonies."

Such devotees attain the astral world on death, only to return back to earth to complete their karmic cycle. Unless, by choice, they choose to attain Moksha-freedom from the cycle of birth and death, and work towards it.

9.22

ananyāś cintayanto māṁ ye janāḥ paryupāsate |
teṣāṁ nityābhiyuktānāṁ yogakṣemaṁ vahāmy aham ||

To men who meditate on Me as their Very Own, ever united to Me by incessant worship, I supply their deficiencies and make permanent their gains.

Explanation:

Once we are aligned with the Supreme path even the smallest details of life are taken care of and aligned. Nature smooths the way so that sincere devotees reach their knowledge potential. Grace is bestowed on sincere seekers, as per the karmic workings of the cosmos.

9.23-24

> ye 'py anyadevatābhaktā yajante śraddhayānvitāḥ |
> te 'pi mām eva kaunteya yajanty avidhipūrvakam ||
>
> ahaṁ hi sarvayajñānāṁ bhoktā ca prabhur eva ca |
> na tu mām abhijānanti tattvenātaś cyavanti te ||

O Son of Kunti (Arjuna), even devotees of other Devas, who sacrifice to them with faith, worship Me alone, though not in the right way.

I am indeed the only Enjoyer and Supreme of all sacrifices. But they (the worshipers of My lesser forms) do not perceive Me in My true nature: hence, they fall.

Explanation:

Persons who worship various deities, are in fact worshipping me alone, as I am their soul, and they, my bodies!

Do we want Brahman or only His gifts? Physical (earth) and Astral (heaven) enjoyments at a sensory level?

If this is what we desire? Do we seek the goal of Self-Realisation and Complete Jnana? A devotee can rise only as high as the object and objective of his worship.

The right way of worship is through yoga meditation that makes us reach a state of samadhi - a state of divine Union with Spirit.

9.25

> yānti devavratā devān pitṛīn yānti pitṛvratāḥ |
> bhūtāni yānti bhūtejyā yānti madyājino 'pi mām ||

Devotees of the astral deities go to them; ancestor worshipers go to the manes: to the nature spirits go those who seek them; but My devotees come to Me.

Explanation:

The gross world is controlled by Devas [subtle energy patterns].

Devas are particular aspect of divinity, who have divine qualities and are very playful. They are present in every cell of your body. These devas can be managed by mantras.

There are 33 kinds of Devas, different patterns of energy to bring comfort to mankind. The 33 Gods mentioned in the Vedas are classified as 12 Adityas, 11 Rudras, 8 Vasus, and 2 Ashvins as per the scriptures. Refer to Chapter 10 & 11

Devas can give us *siddhis* (powers). A *Siddha - Purusha* is a perfected being but does not misuse his powers because he does not desire anything as he has overcome desires.

Praying to Devas and performing rituals bring limited fructification, not eternal liberation and glory. When a person dies, his spirit is not bound. That is why people who are dead can bless you and we seek blessings of ancestors.

Astral deities, ancestors are worshipped by some and get the blessings and benefits from them. The advice here is to seek the whole not a part of the whole.

He says: Those who perform their duties for my sake, depend on me, are devoted to me, are free from attachment and are without malice towards all beings, such devotees certainly come to me.

9.26

patram puṣpam phalam toyam yo me bhaktyā prayacchati |
tad aham bhaktyupahṛtam aśnāmi prayatātmanaḥ ||

The reverent presentation to Me of a leaf, a flower, some fruit, or water, given with pure intention, is a devotional offering acceptable in My sight.

Explanation:

My worship however is very simple. Very little rituals and ingredients are required for it. A few flowers, water and leaves will do. If these offerings are sweetened with whole –hearted devotion, I consume them, as it were eagerly.

Any reverent offering "like the lady Shabri, who tasted every berry checking whether it was sweet enough, before presenting it to me" which is borne out of love reaches me.

The esoteric understanding is that whatever be the stage of spiritual evolution, if the devotee is pure hearted and full of devotion, he achieves divine union.

A leaf is less evolved than a flower; A flower is less evolved than fruit; Yet the simplest of human beings is capable of reaching *Ishvara,* with one-pointed devotion. One may become a seeker at any stage we may be in. Wholehearted devotion is what is the prime ingredient.

9.27-28

yat karoṣi yad aśnāsi yaj juhoṣi dadāsi yat yat |
tapasyasi kaunteya tat kuruṣva madarpaṇam ||

śubhāśubhaphalair evaṁ mokṣyase karmabandhanaiḥ |
saṁnyāsayogayuktātmā vimukto mām upaiṣyasi ||

Whatever actions thou dost perform, O Son of Kunti (Arjuna), whether in eating, or in observing spiritual rites, or in gift bestowing, or in self-disciplining-dedicate them all as offerings to Me.

Thus, no action of thine can enchain thee with good or evil karma. With thy Self steadfastly anchored in Me by Yoga and renunciation, thou shalt win freedom and come unto Me.

Explanation:

In the absolute sense there is no good or evil action. Actions have appropriate results. Good actions will lead to worldly comfort but still bind us to karmic law. We have to consciously move towards result-free, neutral action, karma yoga, free from bondage of karma.

Through steadfast practice of yoga meditation, renunciation of desires and attachments, loving dedication of all actions to the Lord, repentance and right action, not only the righteous attain liberation, even the wicked emerge from ignorance into the healing light of wisdom.

9.29

samo 'haṁ sarvabhūteṣu na me dveṣyo 'sti na priyaḥ |
ye bhajanti tu māṁ bhaktyā mayi te teṣu cāpy aham ||

**I am impartial toward all beings. To Me none is hateful, none is dear.
But those who give Me their heart's love are in Me, as I am in them.**

Explanation:

His rays of sunshine are on everyone, impartially. How much of the sunshine we pick up is up to us. He is impartial and none is dear or hateful. But those who choose love can have Himself in them. (I am in them as they are in me) (refer to 9.4-6)

Nine Types of Bhakti in Dvait sampradaya (tradition):	
Shravana	listening to the glory of the Supreme
Kirtan	singing in his glory
Smaran	constantly thinking about his nature and beauty
Pada Seva	adoring the feet of the Supreme, in a spirit of self-surrender
Archana	worship with the help of sacred mantras and Vedic hymns
Vandana	to pay obeisance to the Supreme
Dasi/Das	serving the Supreme
Sakhya	to invoke him as a friend
Atmanivedana	offer yourself in total surrender

Chart 25

9.30-32

api cet sudurācāro bhajate mām ananyabhāk |
sādhur eva sa mantavyaḥ samyag vyavasito hi saḥ ||

kṣipraṁ bhavati dharmātmā śaśvacchāntiṁ nigacchati |
kaunteya pratijānīhi na me bhaktaḥ praṇaśyati ||

māṁ hi pārtha vyapāśritya ye 'pi syuḥ pāpayonayaḥ |
striyo vaiśyās tathā śūdrās te 'pi yānti parāṁ gatim ||

Even a consummate evildoer who turns away from all else to worship Me exclusively may be counted among the good, because of his righteous resolve.

He will fast become a virtuous man and obtain unending peace. Tell all assuredly, O Arjuna, that My devotee never perishes!

Taking shelter in Me all beings can achieve the Supreme Fulfilment- be they those of sinful birth, or women, or Vaishyas, or Sudras.

Explanation:

Evildoers can turn away anytime from their evil ways and come on to me resulting in purification of the *Antahakaran*. This will make the delusion of the mind disappear and the meditation practices performed after would lead to Jnana.

Antahakaran is our inner instrument- *Chitta, Buddhi Manas Ahamkara*

Purification process can be followed through:	
Fasting	Partaking of food for physical and mental nourishment only
Breath	Balance and energy and detoxification through *Pranayama*
Mind	Thoughts that are always or mostly positive
Tongue	Speech that is always or mostly positive, deliberated and calming

A virtuous man never perishes, as whatever he is seeking, I give onto him as learning and grace resulting in complete fulfilment by becoming a *Jivan Mukta.*

These various diversities of people are mentioned in this one verse.

The caste system became hereditary after the Suryavanshi period, although the varnas were meant to be classified by the inherent characteristics of the person, his inborn talents and his skills as labor.

Lord Krishna again describes the varna classification as Not being based on lineage but on genetic predisposition of *samskara.*

9.33

kiṁ punar brāhmaṇāḥ puṇyā bhaktā rājarṣayas tathā |
anityam asukhaṁ lokam imaṁ prāpya bhajasva mām ||

How easily, then, may I be attained by sainted Brahmins (knowers of Brahman) and pious royal sages (Raja rishis)! Thou who hast entered this impermanent and unhappy world, adore only Me (Spirit).

Explanation:

I can be attained easily by the knowers of Brahman and the *raja rishis.* Realizing his own oneness, the Yogi knows that he himself is a microcosm of immanence and transcendence.

The otherwise impassable gulf between man and his maker, is made possible only thru the science of yoga, which is easy to practice and confers imperishable enlightenment.

9.34

manmanā bhava madbhakto madyājī māṁ namaskuru |
mām evaiṣyasi yuktvaivam ātmānaṁ matparāyaṇaḥ ||

On Me fix thy mind, be thou My devotee, with ceaseless worship. bow reverently before Me. Having thus united thyself to Me as thy Highest Goal, thou shalt be Mine own.

<u>Explanation:</u>

Dedicate as a Yagna all offerings and your ultimate doer-ship of the Ego self. This then makes us free from karmic binding which no normal person can escape. This is liberation or Moksha, freedom from law of Karma and Rebirth.

Complete surrender of Ego (aham) is the greatest of all gifts that one could bestow onto Brahman. However, He is happy to accept the smallest sincere step towards this surrender.

The secret of secrets that Krishna is sharing with us is:

1.	To continue to have the **Wow** factor towards Creation. Brahman itself is Creation and the Creator.
2.	The end and the means to the end is Yoga, the timeless science of Union.
3.	His worship is very simple. very little rituals and ingredients are needed. Only whole-hearted devotion is what is needed.
4.	To realize that the Supreme source is within us.
5.	Brahman is eternal, beginning less, and uncreated, The mortal body is temporary.
6.	Brahman ever was and ever will be, just as finding the beginning of a circle ⬚ is futile.
7.	Omniscient Omnipresent Omnipotent is Divinity.
8.	Let us be loving and caring toward the environment and all living beings.
9.	Perform spiritually strong actions and do not worry or focus on the final outcome of the results
10.	Let us love each other, as the presence of Brahman is in each of his creations. The essence in all of creation is the same Supreme Consciousness. Let us love the entire creation as one family. *(Vasudeva Kutumbakam)*
11.	Renunciate the fruits of action
12.	Peace comes from non-attachment to the material world
13.	Traverse the journey of life with only one destination, Self-realisation
14.	Spiritual wisdom or *Viveka* (keen discernment) is far superior to mechanical rituals or practices.
15.	Intellectual knowledge is necessary but remains theoretical until Meditation secures in us pure intuitional knowledge

Task 6: What is the process by which we can achieve internal purification?

Task 7: Name and describe the types of dvait sampradaya bhakti practices

<u>Summary of Chapter 9</u>

Raja vidya Raja guhiya yoga – Secret science of Raja yoga

Brahman exists without creation, but creation cannot exist without him. He created the universe but does not get involved in it or affected by it. He is in all beings but not in his entirety. Brahman exists in the soul of men, creating and supporting them, yet himself does not get entangled in them.

Brahman is the hidden essence of all manifestation. Nature with her infinite variety and inexorable laws, is an evolute of the singular reality through Cosmic delusion or Maya.

Maya is of the nature of the three qualities of Satva, Rajas and Tamas; and depends on brahman for its existence.

If we see the divine source as a field of unlimited potential, we shall see that Maya created by him is to experience the potential in a field of unlimited possibility! The separation between the creator and his creation becomes *apparent!*

Human reason cannot grasp the meaning of creation…. only intuition can resolve it.

We cannot experience love in astral realm only in the physical. hence human birth is important.

Union with the Absolute Spirit happens when you and He became one—Self-Realisation. This alone permanently uproots the cause of man's threefold suffering of disease, old age, and death.

Human beings though saturated with divinity, are overcome by delusion and made subject to birth and death…a mystery indeed!

We come from the source and our ultimate destiny is to return to that Supreme source.

The intuitive knowledge that comes to us through the energization of the Agya chakra is the Royal Secret of the Raja Rishi's.

Men who cannot perceive the higher purpose of life and do not seek answers, will forever remain trapped in the comings and goings of the earthly cycle.

Our ONLY Dharma is "Self-Realisation"

This highest truth can only be known through personal experience.

An average man is very serious about the worldly spectacle, a Yogi is only serious about knowing God.

To arrive at the ultimate state, one could travel the path of either Karma, Gyana, Raja or Bhakti yoga. The essence of worship is to Know what is to be Known - What is that which is to be known? The Self - by the self. Ultimate worship is this secret.

Krishna says, "The small pleasures on the earthly plane I shall grant you through rituals, Pooja's, havans, homas and other vedic fire ceremonies."

A devotee can rise only as high as the object and objective of his worship.

The right way of worship is through yoga meditation that makes us reach a samadhi state of divine Union with Spirit.

Complete Soul surrender is the greatest of all gifts that one could bestow. However, He is happy to accept the smallest sincere step towards this surrender.

Once we are aligned with the universal path even the smallest details of life are taken care of. Nature smooths the way so that sincere devotees reach their knowledge potential.

We are exactly halfway through the Gita's 18 chapters. Chapter 9 is the exact center where this secret is unveiled.

The mystery disclosed in Chapter 9 is that there is nothing out there in the skies or in the heavens to reach for or try to attain. We must reach into the self to reach the SELF.

The karmic pattern (or samskaras / vasanas) are created by man himself through misuse or good use of free will choice.

Here Krishna says that the secret to attain wisdom and release the self from suffering is to turn one's action into surrender, prayers, and offerings to the cosmos and its innate intelligence. *Vivek,* Wisdom, *Jnana, Dhyana,* Knowledge, Discriminative intellect, *Buddhi* are all the subtle instruments for gaining spiritual knowledge. We get strength from spirituality in all seasons of life.

Intuitively and spiritually, we seek these answers, as our full potential can only be be achieved with total and complete knowledge, *Gyana.* We should start young, as we grow older our faculties decline.

The cosmos operates on the principle of karma and therefore everyone is just as they ought to be and experiencing exactly their own reality.

Krishna imparts the knowledge of 'devotion' and moving beyond knowing and feeling the vibration of divinity in every experience. By pure devotion, we will be released from the bondage of karmas and attain the goal of mystic union Yuj.

Realizing this with rightful worship and with utmost devotion, we attain union by turning actions into prayers.

Comments by nascent students' study of Bhakti yoga:

Brahman is beyond time. Ever now (Ever present) When Ishvara dreams, Creation happens.

The unmanifested Spirit is Consciousness divided into a 3-part trinity **Aum - Tat - Sat**

SAT is the Supreme Spirit which exists beyond the vibratory dream creation, ever-existing, Changeless, All inclusive, Imperishable.

TAT or Kutastha Chaitanya, Brahman's Pure reflection, omnipresent in creation.

Brahman's essence is Sat - Chit - Anand

Brahman is both within and beyond the Universe. Simultaneously pervading it and surpassing it.

The Gita is not only a Moksha Shastra, but also teaches how to live in a righteous way, teaches us the essence of Dharma

Gita teaches us to get rid of *samskara* and *vasanas by antahakaran shuddhi* and becoming a *Sthit Pragya* person like a Yogi who is firmly established in Supreme Consciousness.

Union – Yog can be attained by - Practice of Divine science of Yoga with a focused mind, a heart full of devotion, Surrendering Ego, Sacrificing all Fruits of action and by constant remembrance of the Supreme Source.

Restfulness' occurs with deep insight into the mind with the help of yoga to remove monkey mind chatter and for tuning into intuition.

Task 8 for the reader: What is the secret of all secrets that Sri Krishna is sharing with us?

Om   Creative Vibration

Tat   Ishvara or Kutastha Chaitanya

Sat   Brahman

BHAGAVAD GITA VOLUME – 2

Chapter 10

Vibhuti Yoga

The Infinite Manifestations of The Unmanifest Spirit

Introduction to Chapter 10

This chapter describes the all-pervasive power and presence of the Divine. This chapter is termed as Vibhuti Yoga - depicting the attributes of Brahman that declare his all-pervading manifestations of which we are one too.

In this chapter Arjuna realizes the vastness of Brahman, who is the imperishable, the eternal infinite, the ever present, unbound, unrelated to time and space.

Although there is multiplicity evident all around us in the universe, there is an underlying Oneness. There is identity [oneness] between the Microcosm and the Macrocosm. The part is never separate from the whole. It is always inherent in the whole.

The individual mind is part of the total mind. Similarly, the individual gross body [*Pinda*] is part of the total gross body *[Brahmand].* The individual and total enjoy a part-whole relationship. *Jiva atman* is not separate from *Param atman.*

Brahman is the eternal consciousness, unchanging and indivisible, in which the illusions of time [change] and space [division] present an infinite variety of forms interacting in a progressive mode of past, present and future.

"The apparent multiplication of God is bewildering at first glance but soon we discover that these Gods are all the same God in different aspects and functions. There is always an uttermost (*uttam*) God that defies personification. This makes Hinduism the most tolerant religion in the world as its one transcendent God includes all possible Gods". - Sir George Bernard Shaw.

There is an underlying oneness underlying the multiplicity! *YOU* are the non-dual reality as per the Vedas. Investigate the present reality and awareness and everything appears to Awareness! Deeper investigation shows us that isness and awareness just appear to be different but are all the same.

Once we realize this, it takes away all suffering and brings bliss. There is no second reality apart from this.

The entire universe is a divine manifestation in all its diversity. Brahman is both beyond Creation [Sat] and in creation [Tat]. *Ekam Sat*: is the unifying essence running through all experiences and all expressions of life and matter.

Those who are born are controlled by *maya,* the three *gunas* and the dualities of nature. One must use one's discrimination and free will choice to first understand and then uplift us from this play of *maya*, to be in union with Divine vibration.

He (Brahman) is the best of the best, just as we strive to be! We will read the following verses in duality (*dvait*) as - He (Brahman) and his powers vs Me (man) and *maya.*

Awaken in knowledge - Arise!

Macrocosm – The Whole		**Microcosm** – Part of the Whole
Brahmand	Gross body	*Pinda*
Param atman	*Atman / spirit*	*Jiva atman*

Chart 26

10

Vibhuti Yoga – The Infinite Manifestations of The Unmanifest Spirit

10.1-3

Srī Bhagavān uvāca:

bhūya eva mahābāho śṛṇu me paramaṁ vacaḥ |
yat te 'haṁ prīyamāṇāya vakṣyāmi hitakāmyayā ||

na me viduḥ suragaṇāḥ prabhavaṁ na maharṣayaḥ |
aham ādir hi devānāṁ maharṣīṇāṁ ca sarvaśaḥ ||

yo mām ajam anādiṁ ca vetti lokamaheśvaram |
asaṁmūḍhaḥ sa martyeṣu sarvapāpaiḥ pramucyate ||

The Blessed Lord said:

O Mighty-Armed (Arjuna), hear thou more of My utterances. For thy highest good I will speak further to thee, who listeneth joyfully.

Neither the multitude of angels nor the great sages know My Uncreated Nature, for even the devas and rishis (are created beings, and hence) have an origin in Me.

But whoever realizes Me to be the Unborn and Beginningless, as well as the Sovereign of Creation-that man has conquered delusion and attained the sinless state even while wearing a mortal body.

Explanation:

Reaching the Source is reaching the Self because the *Atman* pervading within the *jiva* is the same *Ishvara* or Supreme source of Creation - Brahman.

Here Krishna begins by expounding the origin of Creation-Brahman. Whatever has become manifested after Creation cannot understand or fathom what Is /Was before manifestation. The Devi-Devas, The Rishis and sages have all been created by Brahman.

For us to fathom the unmanifested nature of Brahman - that field of unlimited potential, we have to be pure of heart, pure of mind and pure of intellect and above any delusion.

The tenth chapter of the Gita is called ***Vibhuti Yoga,*** which describes the glory and opulence's of God:

The power of the Self
The pervasiveness of the Self
The Self as the essence in the world of plurality

Chart 27

In this chapter the Divine indicates himself both as:

The most prominent and chief factor in all classes of beings.
The supreme factor without which specimens belonging to each class cannot maintain themselves as existent beings.

Chart 28

We are seeing the confused man of indecision revealed in Chapter 1 (Arjuna *Vishad*) now developing an almost incomparable inward equipoise.

He asks Arjuna who is very dear to Him, to listen to his words carefully for his own spiritual welfare.

When one comes to know that the Best of Best in him, this world, and universe belongs to Brahman, his Ego gets nullified.

As everything is Ishvara there are no personal accomplishments; this knowledge takes us above *raga-dvesa* and aids us in self-purification (antaha-karan-shuddhi) and diminishes the might of the personal *ahamkara* - ego.

He says As I am the source of all demigods and sages, so it is not possible for them even to know me completely. Ishvara is the cause of all causes. The pure consciousness is the source or the substratum for both physical and astral life in each one of us.

Consciousness being the very subjective truth in us can never become the object of perception (for senses), object of feeling for the mind, or an object of knowing for the intellect.

The man who realizes or rediscovers the nature of the self and gains thereby a perfect and complete identification with self can no longer suffer the pain of bondage. He is liberated, as He is Akarta. Such a man knows the self as eternal.

Everything else is born in the Self, exists in the Self and all ends in the Self. So, he is eternal and causeless, means the one who has no cause but he himself is the cause of everything. This Self is the great Lord of all the worlds (*Sarva Loka Maheshwaram*), the Supreme Self is experiencing Creation through the Macrocosm.

10.4-5

buddhir jñānam asaṁmohaḥ kṣamā satyaṁ damaḥ śamaḥ |
sukhaṁ duḥkhaṁ bhavo 'bhāvo bhayaṁ cābhayaṁ eva ca ||

ahiṁsā samatā tuṣṭis tapo dānaṁ yaśo 'yaśaḥ |
bhavanti bhāvā bhūtānāṁ matta eva pṛthagvidhāḥ ||

Discrimination, wisdom, lack of delusion, forgiveness, truth, control of the senses, peace of mind, joy, sorrow, birth, death, fear and courage.

Harmlessness, equanimity, serenity, self-discipline, charity, fame, and infamy-these diverse states of being's spring from Me alone as modifications of My nature.

<u>Explanation:</u>

20 Modifications of Human nature described by Krishna:

Discrimination	Control of the senses	Truth	Charity
Wisdom	Peace of mind	Joy	Death
Lack of delusion	Birth	Serenity	Fear
Forgiveness	Courage	Self-discipline	Sorrow
Harmlessness	Equanimity	Fame	Infamy

Verse 4 and 5 say – *Ishvara* is the Supreme of all beings because *He* possesses all the qualities of living beings. He is the material and efficient cause of the world of plurality within and without an individual. Nothing can manifest itself in this material world, which is not Him.

Here he expresses various qualities of the mind and intellect whether good or bad which come from Him alone. Brahman is the complete classification of an entire world of beings and their fields of experiences.

Some of the qualities which are depicted and characterized in the numerous stories of the Pandavas in the Mahabattle are: Intellect, wisdom, non-delusion, forgiveness, self-restraint, calmness, happiness, pain, fear, fearlessness, equanimity, contentment, austerity, fame, infamy, truth…etc.

10.6

maharṣayaḥ sapta pūrve catvāro manavas tathā |
madbhāvā mānasā jātā yeṣāṁ loka imāḥ prajāḥ ||

the seven great rishis, the primeval four, and the (fourteen) manus are also modifications of my nature, born of my thought, and endowed with (creative) powers like mine, from these progenitors come all living creatures on earth.

Explanation:

I am the cause of *sages, sanat kumaras and manus.* The seven *Rishis*, the *Manus* and the *Sanat kumaras* were born by My Mind, by mere *sankalpa* and from them the creatures of the world originated and were sustained.

Krishna is limitless and infinite whereas individual self *(jivatma)* is limited and finite. This has been confirmed by the great sages and seers such as Vyasa, Vasistha, and Parasara.

Esoteric Explanation:

The Seven Rishis are personified representatives of the seven seers and are nothing but one's intellect, ego and the five sense stimuli.

The Macrocosmic projection of a created Universe through the 7 seers (**sapta rishis**) is the Lord's own Vibhuti (glory), while the Microcosmic experience of the world through our mind born qualities of prakriti, is through individual consciousness.

Sanat Kumars are the **4 sons of Brahma** and are the eternal qualities of *prakriti* as ever youthful, ancient, joyous and eternal.

The **Manus** who are the progenitors of the human race, formulated the laws of behavior in personal life and in society, leading us to becoming decent people as members of family, of the community, of the nation and of the world.

The seven great **Rishis** and fourteen **Manus** are the progenitors of the human race:

Brahma, and his four sons:	
1. Sanaka	From the beginning
2. Sanananda	Consciousness of Bliss
3. Sanatana	Eternal, Everlasting
4. Sanat kumara	Ever Young
The seven (sapt) Rishis 1. Marichi 2. Atri 3. Angiras 4. Pulaha 5. Kratir 6. Pulastya 7. Vashishtha	Divine beings said to be liberated in spirit during the Solar Age, to whom the Vedas were revealed. They represent the 7 principles of life and consciousness.

And from the lineage of **14 Manus** (fathers of mankind) all beings descend.		
1. Svayambhu 2. Svarocisa 3. Uttama 4. Tamasa 5. Raivata 6. Chakshusa	7. **Vivasvat** 8. Savarni 9. Daksha-savarni 10. Brahma-savarni 11. Dharma-savarni 12. Rudra-savarni 13. Deva-savarini 14. Indra savarini	The seventh Manu **Vivasvat** [Sun-born], is the progenitor of the present race.
Each successive Manu is associated with a particular cycle of manifestation and dissolution		

Chart 29

10.7-8

etāṁ vibhūtiṁ yogaṁ ca mama yo vetti tattvataḥ |
so 'vikampena yogena yujyate nātra saṁśayaḥ ||

ahaṁ sarvasya prabhavo mattaḥ sarvaṁ pravartate |
iti matvā bhajante māṁ budhā bhāvasamanvitāḥ ||

He who realizes by yoga the truth of My prolific manifestations, and the creative and dissolving power of My Divine Yoga is unshakably united to Me. This is beyond doubt.

I am the Source of everything; from Me all creation emerges. With this Realisation the wise, awestricken, adore Me.

"He who knows My glories and My yogic power gets established in knowledge, which is unshakable".

Explanation:

The one who knows his vibhuti – (opulence's / glories), and how they come about, and their connection, gets an unshakeable vision of the Self.

Understanding Ishvara means understanding the whole *jagat* as Ishvara. Knowledge is to be realized in a subjective experience and intuitively lived as 'I am the Self'.

In the next verse He elaborates on how we could be steadily and permanently established in the infinite Self.

10.9

maccittā madgataprāṇā bodhayantaḥ parasparam |

kathayantaś ca māṁ nityaṁ tuṣyanti ca ramanti ca ||

Their thoughts fully on Me, their beings surrendered to Me, enlightening one another, proclaiming Me always, my devotees are contented and joyful.

Explanation:

Pure devotees, engage themselves fully in the loving service of the Supreme Source.

Bhakti: is the love, devotion, learning and yearning of wanting to surrender oneself completely and selflessly to become one with Cosmic Consciousness. Nothing else remains to be achieved or sought. Faith creates such a quality in our consciousness that it makes it solid and stable, faith brings totality. Doubt makes the mind unstable and causes dissemination of energy. Faith integrates your whole personality, there is consolidation of energy. When there is faith, Samadhi can be achieved.

10.10-11

> teṣāṁ satatayuktānāṁ bhajatāṁ prītipūrvakam |
> dadāmi buddhiyogaṁ taṁ yena māṁ upayānti te ||
>
> teṣām evānukampārtham aham ajñānajaṁ tamaḥ |
> nāśayāmy ātmabhāvastho jñānadīpena bhāsvatā ||

To those thus ever attached to Me, and who worship Me with love, I impart that discriminative wisdom (buddhi yoga) by which they attain Me utterly.

From sheer compassion I, the Divine Indweller, set alight in them the radiant lamp of wisdom which banishes the darkness that is born of ignorance.

Explanation:

To those who are constantly devoted to worship Me with love, I give the understanding by which they can come to Me.

To show them special mercy, I, dwelling in their hearts, destroy with the shining lamp of knowledge the darkness born of ignorance. Without discriminating intelligence, one cannot have pure knowledge.

For them this answer is given by the Self: those who are devoted to him, even though they be without sufficient education and even without sufficient knowledge of the Vedic principles, are still helped by Brahman, as stated in this verse.

In this verse the word buddhi-yoga is very significant.

In the second chapter Krishna, whilst instructing Arjuna, said that He had spoken to him of many things and that He would now instruct him in the way of *Buddhi-yoga*.

Buddhi Yoga: Is the devotion through which a disciple gains that wisdom which sees Brahman in all forms that change and pass.

Buddhi means intelligence, and yoga means activities for union and elevation. Buddhi-yoga is the process by which one gets out of the entanglement of this material world. We understand the true nature of the Self through absolute devotion to the Supreme consciousness, and merge with Him.

Brahman creates the world for man's welfare, Himself remaining apart from it. Devotion leads to removal of the veil of ignorance and when ignorance is destroyed, Brahman stands revealed to the human spirit.

<u>10.12-13</u>

Arjuna uvāca:

paraṁ brahma paraṁ dhāma pavitraṁ paramaṁ bhavān |
puruṣaṁ śāśvataṁ divyam ādidevam ajaṁ vibhum ||

āhus tvām ṛṣayaḥ sarve devarṣir nāradas tathā |
asito devalo vyāsaḥ svayaṁ caiva bravīṣi me ||

Arjuna said:

The Supreme Spirit, the Supreme Shelter, the Supreme Purity art Thou! All the great sages, the divine seer Narada, as well as Asita Devala, and Vyasa, have thus described Thee as the Self-Evolved Eternal Being, the Original Deity, uncaused and omnipresent. And now Thou Thyself tellest me!

<u>Explanation:</u>

<u>Arjuna</u> said: You are the Supreme Personality of Godhead, the ultimate abode, the purest, the Absolute Truth. You are the eternal, transcendental, original person, the unborn, the greatest.

All the great sages such as <u>Narada</u>, <u>Asita</u>, <u>Devala</u> and <u>Vyasa</u> confirm this truth about You, and now You Yourself are declaring it to me.

These verses are important because Brahman Himself is declaring the truth of his Omnipotence here! He is confirming what the great seers and rishis have been telling us.

<u>Refer to the detailed Glossary at the end of Chapter 10</u>

10.14

> sarvam etad ṛtaṁ manye yan māṁ vadasi keśava |
> na hi te bhagavan vyaktiṁ vidur devā na dānavāḥ ||

O Keshava (Krishna)! I consider as eternal truth all Thou hast revealed to me. Indeed, O my Supreme! neither the Devas (gods) nor the Danavas (Titans) know the infinite modes of Thine appearances.

Explanation:

O Krishna, I totally accept as truth all that You have told me. Neither the demigods nor the giants, understand your personality.

The acceptance by Arjuna of all that Krishna says could be emulated to understand the essence of Bhagavad Gita.

The ray of devotion is not different from the ray of knowledge called *jnana*. When intelligence matures and lodges securely in the mind it becomes wisdom. When wisdom is integrated with life it expresses in our action and becomes *bhakti*.

Knowledge when fully matured is *bhakti*, if *gyana* does not get transformed into *bhakti* such knowledge is useless tinsel.

To believe that jnana and *bhakti*, knowledge and devotion are different from each other is ignorance.

Sage Adi Shankaracharya himself, who drank the ocean of knowledge as easily as the 1/5th cup of water in the palm of his hand, sang devotional hymns in his later years to develop bhakti and love for the divine. This is enough to show us that *jnana and bhakti* are one and the same.

The varied *bhavas* [attitudes/ emotions] a devotee takes according to his temperament to express his devotion towards God are:

1	*Santa*	placid love for God
2	*Dasya*	attitude of a servant
3	*Sakhya*	the attitude of a friend
4	*Vatsala*	the attitude of a mother to her child
5	*Madhurya*	The attitude of a woman towards her lover

10.15-16

svayam evātmanātmānaṁ vettha tvaṁ puruṣottama |
bhūtabhāvana bhūteśa devadeva jagatpate ||

vaktum arhasy aśeṣeṇa divyā hy ātmavibhūtayaḥ |
yābhir vibhūtibhir lokān imāṁs tvaṁ vyāpya tiṣṭhasi ||

O Divine Purusha, O Origin of beings, O the Lord of all creatures, O God of Gods, O Sustainer of the world! verily Thou alone knowest Thyself by Thyself.

Therefore, please tell me exhaustively of Thy divine powers and qualities by which Thine Omnipresence sustaineth the cosmos.

Explanation:

Arjuna continues to ask Krishna and, in the process, confirms the opinion of sages/ rishis and whatever he has learnt, so far, that Krishna is Ishvara. Then he asks Krishna to talk about all his glories, by which He remains immanent in the entire universe, as Krishna himself is the most eligible one to talk about it.

10.17

kathaṁ vidyām ahaṁ yogiṁs tvāṁ sadā paricintayan |
keṣu keṣu ca bhāveṣu cintyo 'si bhagavan mayā ||

O Great Yogi (Krishna)! How shall I always meditate to know Thee truly? In what aspects and forms, O Blessed Bhagavan, art Thou to be conceived by me?

Explanation:

Also, Arjuna wants to know how he can meditate on Him. He is manifest in everything but the glories of some objects and people stand out in creation.

Arjuna wants to know the objects in which he can see the glory of Ishvara.

Arjuna is yet not fully satiated and still craves to hear the grandeur of Krishna, in his nectar like sweet words.

10.18-20

vistareṇātmano yogaṁ vibhūtiṁ ca janārdana |
bhūyaḥ kathaya tṛptir hi śṛṇvato nāsti me 'mṛtam ||

Srī Bhagavān uvāca:

hanta te kathayiṣyāmi divyā hy ātmavibhūtayaḥ |
prādhānyataḥ kuruśreṣṭha nāsty anto vistarasya me ||

aham ātmā guḍākeśa sarvabhūtāśayasthitaḥ ||
aham ādiś ca madhyaṁ ca bhūtānām anta eva ca ||

O Janardana (Krishna)! Tell me more, at great length, of Thy yoga powers and Self manifestations; for never can I hear enough of Thy nectared speech!

The Blessed Krishna said:

Very well, O Best of the Princes (Arjuna), I will indeed tell thee of My phenomenal expressions but only the most outstanding ones, for there is no end to My variety.

O Conqueror of Sleep (Arjuna)! I am the Self in the heart of all creatures: I am their Origin, Existence, and Finality.

Explanation:

To this Krishna replies that His manifestations are endless, but He can enumerate a few, which are of prominence.

Ishvara is the beginning, middle and end of every being. He is the cause for creation, sustenance, and dissolution. Ishvara can be invoked in any given form, in any object that has some glory. [e.g. sugar in sugarcane, sweetness of sugar is Ishvara].

There are countless names and forms, all of which are available for meditation. In Chapter 7, it was said that He is the essence of everything—*rasa in water, tej in agni* etc.

The main point here is, that an object is, what it is, because of glory of Ishvara. Whatever in this creation is of value, of prominence, is all sustained by Him and reflects glory of Ishvara.

He addresses Arjuna as the <u>conqueror of sleep</u> and its esoteric meaning is the one who conquers ignorance and delusion.

In this verse He begins the description of His manifestations by declaring that He is the creator, sustainer and destroyer of all

In these verses 21 through 39 the He is describing His glories and in those who possess these extraordinary, exalted glories/virtues, His power is present in them in a greater degree.

God is that consciousness, which is free of Kalesha [misery], Karma, Vipaka [fruit of action] and Ashaya [latent desires or opinions].

The 16 Glories /*Kalas* of Lord Krishna

Daya	compassion	*Danasheel*	Benevolent, bestower of all wealth in the world and nature
Dhairya	Patience	*Saundarya maya*	Beauty incarnate
Kshama	Forgiveness	*Nrityajna*	Best of dancers
Nyaya	Justice	*Sangitajna*	Best of musicians
Nirapeksha	Impartiality	*Neetivadi*	Embodiment of honesty
Nirasakta	Detachment	*Satyavadi*	Truth itself
Tapasya	Meditation and Spiritual Powers	*Sarvagnata*	All-knowing
Aparchitta	Invincibility	*Sarvaniyanta*	Controller of All.

The Six-fold opulence's attributed to Ishvara are:

Shree	Absolute Wealth
Yash	Absolute Fame
Aishwarya	Absolute Lordship and Beauty
Virya	Absolute Strength and Power
Jnana	Absolute Knowledge
Vairagya	Absolute Detachment

Chart 30

10.21

ādityānām ahaṁ viṣṇur jyotiṣāṁ ravir aṁśumān |
marīcir marutām asmi nakṣatrāṇām ahaṁ śaśī ||

Among the Adityas (twelve effulgent beings), I am Vishnu; among luminaries, I am the radiating sun; among the Maruts (forty-nine wind gods), I am Marichi; among heavenly bodies, I am the moon.

The Twelve Adityas (effulgent beings)

1	Aryaman	7	Vivasvat
2	Indra	8	Amsa
3	Tvastr	9	Mitra
4	Varuna	10	Pusan
5	Bhaga	11	Daksha
6	Savitr	12	**Vishnu**

Chart 31

Explanation:

The entire universe is a divine manifestation of Brahman in all its diversities. Brahman is both beyond creation [**Sat**] and in creation [**Tat**]

Luminaries: His glory is expressed as the radiating **Sun**

Maruts: The 49 wind gods are named in the glossary at end of this chapter. He is **Marichi,** the mightiest amongst the presiding deities of the storms (maruts). In the body of man there are 7 principal life current vortexes (7 chakras) that are amplified into 49 special life forces – Maruts.

Amongst the Heavenly bodies: He is the moon.

From verse 10.19 onwards He starts explaining about his glories to Arjuna which is also the name of the chapter *Vibuthi* yoga. Verses 10.22 to 28 continue in the same vein:

10.22

vedānāṁ sāmavedo 'smi devānām asmi vāsavaḥ |
indriyāṇāṁ manaś cāsmi bhūtānām asmi cetanā ||

Among the Vedas, I am the Sama Veda; among the Gods, I am Vasava (Indra); among the senses, I am mind (manas); in creatures, I am the intelligence.

Explanation:

Krishna says amongst the **Vedas**, He is the **Sama veda**. Even though all Vedas talk about his glories, Sama veda stands out among the other Vedas as it is recited in a musical form and has the famous mahavakya "TAT TVAM ASI". He says, I am the infinite essence of music in the Samaveda.

He is **Vasava** (the deity **Indra**) among *devas* (gods). Vasava (Indra) is the Lord of *Devas*.

Amongst the **senses**, I am the **Mind**, as the mind is what controls our sense organs. The **Manas (mind)** is the coordinator of the 10 senses. Therefore, it is powerful as a controller.

The inner being in everyone is the Atman and it is not contaminated. The mind worships its being and when the boundary of ignorance collapses, it becomes infinite. We pray to this infinite being that we are. Worship is an act of dissolving the mind into being that which is free from misery. It becomes the same as the divine that rules the universe!

He is the **Intelligence** amongst embodied beings – the capacity to inquire, seek, know and understand. **Intelligence** is also powerful when its discriminatory sense of making the right choices of turning away from short term pleasures is active.

10.23

rudrāṇāṁ śaṁkaraś cāsmi vitteśo yakṣarakṣasām |
vasūnāṁ pāvakaś cāsmi meruḥ śikhariṇām aham ||

Of the Rudras (eleven radiant beings), I am (their leader) Shankara ("the well-wisher"); of the Yakshas and Rakshasas (astral demi-goblins), I am Kubera (Deva of riches), of the Vasus (eight vitalizing beings), I am Pavaka (the God of fire, the purifying power); and of mountain peaks, I am Meru.

<u>Explanation:</u>

I am Shankara among *Rudras* – (*Rudra* is the deity of destruction, also known as Shiva, the destroyer, who destroys ignorance, is the ruler of transformation and is worshipped for attaining *Moksha*). There are 11 Rudras. He is the Lord of all manifestations and dissolutions.

Shankara is the ultimate Rudra as there is nothing superior to Moksha.

<u>Refer to glossary at the end of chapter.</u>

He continues, I am *Kubera* the presiding deity of wealth among the *yakshas.* (Lakshmi is the Goddess of wealth, and Kubera is her keeper of the wealth). *Rakshasas* are demons.

I am fire among the 8 <u>Vasus</u> because by burning He purifies everything, here we can say purification of mind. <u>Pavaka is the God of Fire.</u>

I am *Meru* among the snow peaked mountains.

The Eight Vasus

1	Dyaus	Sky
2	Prithvi	Earth
3	Vayu	Wind
4	Agni	fire
5	Nakshatras	Stars
6	Varuna	Water
7	Surya	Sun
8	Chandra	Moon

<u>Chart 32</u>

10.24

purodhasāṁ ca mukhyaṁ māṁ viddhi pārtha bṛhaspatim |
senānīnām ahaṁ skandaḥ sarasām asmi sāgaraḥ ||

And, O son of Pritha (Arjuna), understand Me to be the chief among priests, Brihaspati; among generals, I am Skanda; among expanses of water, I am the ocean.

Explanation:

I am **Brihaspati,** the chief among priest (He is the guru of Indra and so even Indra bows to Brihaspati).

I am **Skanda** or Subrahmanya who is the general of Devas. He is the Son of Shiva and is invoked for protection from any type of fear. Skanda is the son of Shiva, Kartikeyan representing 'Self-control', the leading warrior of our discriminative faculties of buddhi/intellect in its fight with our sense bound manas/mind, led by the Manipur Chakra.

Among the **water reservoirs** I am the mighty **ocean.** Amongst the expanses of water, He is the vast ocean.

10.25

maharṣīṇāṁ bhṛgur ahaṁ girām asmy ekam akṣaram |
yajñānāṁ japayajño 'smi sthāvarāṇāṁ himālayaḥ ||

Of the Maharishis (mighty sages), I am Bhrigu; among words, I am the one syllable Aum: among yajnas (holy ceremonies), I am japa-yajna (silent, superconscious chanting); among stationary objects, I am the Himalaya.

Explanation:

Among the **sages (maharishis),** I am **Bhrigu** as he is considered the greatest (He is the son of Manu, and he got his knowledge from his father).

Among **words** he is the most powerful one syllable AUM. I am the single word syllable **Aum** representing all words. 'A' stands for the waking of the world, 'U' stands for the thought of the world and 'M' for the unmanifest.

Aum starts with the creation (*srishti*) and resolves into Brahman. OM is thus a word or symbol for meditation upon Param Brahman. It is a universal sound consisting of 3 sounds. When anyone opens his/her mouth and makes a sound, it is 'a'. When he closes his mouth and makes a sound, 'm' is the sound produced. The same 'a' becomes 'u' when mouth is rounded.

These are the sounds which come naturally to any human being. All words are combinations of these sounds. **Aum,** as a word means that which protects and sustains everything, which is none other than *Ishvara.* Aum is also the cosmic vibratory intelligence.

Yajna's or Yagyas are holy ceremonies performed in surrender as oblations or offerings. Among rituals I am *Japa*, when we chant *(japa)* aurally or conduct mental repetition of the Ishvara's name, we bind our mind in concentration. This leads to a focused and one pointed thread of devotion that results in sanctifying the mind.

Japayagna - is also super conscious chanting in silence, hearing the inner divine sound through perception of the purifying vibration of the holy OM. When you are in that state of consciousness, you undergo transformation-you become a witness and all obstacles to reaching the divine source are removed.

Among **stationary objects** I am the **Himalayas** (the vastest of all mountain ranges).

10.26

asvatthah sarvavrksanam devarsinam ca naradah |
gandharvanam citrarathah siddhanam kapilo munih ||

Among all trees, I am the Ashvattha (the holy fig tree); among the deva rishis (divine sages), I am Narada; among the Gandharvas, (demigods),

I am Chitraratha; among the siddhas (successful liberated beings), I am the muni (saint) Kapila.

Explanation:

Narada is a deva rishi and is considered a completely liberated soul.

Among siddhas I am Sage Kapila, as he is one of the great thinkers and is the author of Sankhya philosophy. The concept of One Truth, Absolute and Eternal is the same school of thought and Sage Kapila has been given the special glory of being compared to the Divine.

Refer to complete glossary at end of chapter 10

10.27

uccaiḥśravasam aśvānāṁ viddhi māṁ amṛtodbhavam |
airāvataṁ gajendrāṇāṁ narāṇāṁ ca narādhipam ||

Among stallions, know Me to be the nectar-born. Uchchaihshravas; among elephants, Indra's white elephant, Airavata; and among men, the emperor.

Explanation:

Horse: carrying the mind to the Spirit on the current of life force, Prana

Uchai-Shravas: A rushing stream from high above the Uplifting Life current. Also called the upward soaring Stallion 🐎 of the Sun ☀

In all these examples it is clear that the Divine is indicating Himself to be the paramount, that he is transcendent and omnipotent.

In the puranic story, when *Amrut - Manthan* (churning of the ocean) takes place, thirteen tempting objects come forth.

Of these two were the horse named *Uchaishravas,* and the elephant named *Airavata.*

Elephants are a symbol of wisdom - and Indra is the conqueror of the इंद्रिय (Senses), Both were presented to the King of the Devas, Indra.

10.28

āyudhānām ahaṁ vajraṁ dhenūnām asmi kāmadhuk |
prajanaś cāsmi kandarpaḥ sarpāṇām asmi vāsukiḥ ||

Among weapons, I am the thunderbolt Vajra; of bovines, I am Kamadhuk (the celestial cow that fulfils all desires). I am Kandarpa (the personified creative consciousness), the cause of childbirths: and I am Vasuki among serpents.

Explanation:

Vajra is a weapon in the divine artillery that cannot be destroyed.

Kamdhuk is also a product of the *Amrut-Manthan* (churning of the ocean), a cow from which we can milk and gratify all desires.

Kandarpa, the God of love, Cupid, represents, in the field of sensuality, satisfaction of all the three sheaths of Man- physical, mental and intellectual.

Kamadhuk or *Kamadhenu* - is a celestial cow ⍰- the fulfiller of all wishes; she is symbolic of divine wisdom, nourishing whom satisfies all physical, mental, and spiritual longings.

Kamadeva is The Deva of desire and love, also referred to as *Kandarpa*, creative consciousness that begets children through the act of sexual consummation.

Vasuki is symbolic of the coiled *Kundalini* serpent. (Swami Chinmayananda interprets that Vasuki is a serpent that is small compared to the Nagas which are big (in the next stanza).

10.29

anantaś cāsmi nāgānaṁ varuṇo yādasām aham |
pitṛīṇām aryamā cāsmi yamaḥ saṁyamatām aham ||

I am *Ananta* ("the eternal" one) among the *Naga* serpents; I am *Varuna* (Brahman of the ocean) among water creatures; I am *Aryama* among *Pitris* (ancestral parents); I am *Yama* (Lord of death) among all controllers.

Explanation:

Here he gives detailed examples of his glorious attributes...

Amongst the great serpents, He is **Ananta.**

Ananta is the force of Cosmic Delusion, those forces of Maya that bemuse Creation. *Ananta* is the Shesh Nag which remains even when is in a state of suspension.

Ananta: the eternal non-poisonous serpent or <u>shesha naga</u> on whose head rests, like a mustard seed, the entire infinite range of universes! Also, in his Yogic sleep Vishnu (sustainer) and Brahma (creator) or Illusion maker rests on.

Shesha means, "that which remains" or the entire preserved map of the potential of creation (a blueprint) which is suspended in between during the *maha pralaya* and what can symbolically be explained as the cosmic delusion of creation *(Maya).* The consciousness of Spirit which forms the universe.

I am also the Lord of water and all the beings in the ocean **Varuna,** a deity which is depicted as being a merman (half man half fish)

I am also *Aryama* who is the chief of all ancestors or the parent of all parents. The one who carried the master seed like Adam. Aryama is the chief Aditya (from 6-12 of them) who are the upholders of the Law of time,12 months of the year like the spokes on the wheel of time! They are also considered to be the 12 shining sons of Surya. They live in the astral world of ancestors or Pitri loka and are the sons of Aditi.

Aryama is the Creative light of the Astral World and the Chief of all ancestors *(pitris).*

And *Yama* the deva of death, symbolically means self-control and the power to govern oneself, in our passage to either a brighter or darker world depending on our Karma. Without death we cannot have life, so it is as powerful as creation itself.

Example: To have the ability to do anything one has to first destroy what is and then create a new canvas.

10.30

> prahlādaś cāsmi daityānāṁ kālaḥ kalayatām aham |
> mṛgāṇāṁ ca mṛgendro 'haṁ vainateyaś ca pakṣiṇām ||

Among the Daityas (demons and giants), I am Prahlada; among measurers, I am time; among the animals, I am the king of beasts (the lion); and among birds, I am Garuda (Supreme of the skies, the vehicle of Vishnu).

<u>Explanation:</u>

Even amongst *Daityas* (**demons and giants)** who were the off springs of *Diti,* the opposite of Aditi, I am *Prahlada,* who despite having demonic parents steadfastly worshipped the Lord, and is an example to all. Symbolically **Prahlada** is the one who can master delusion- bound forces in our body and reverse the flow upward towards the Sahasrara.

Amongst those who measure, I am **time,** the eternal infinite unstoppable time. The illusion of time appears to change and be divided into space. But in a dream, there is no space or time only a consciousness. I am that consciousness which just is without being restricted by the divisions of space and changes of time.

Brahman is the eternal consciousness, unchanging and indivisible, in which the illusions of **time** [change] and space [division] present an infinite variety of forms interacting in a progressive mode of past, present and future.

The concepts of time and space are both man-made distinctions. These are suggested by Nature's power of illusion and applied to the changes happening around us. There is really no past, present or future. What we have is just the Now and our awareness of the Now moment. That Now moment is all of existence. Everything else is a play of the mind (maya) alone.

Amongst animals the mighty **Lion.** Amongst birds I am their **King Garuda,** the vehicle of Lord Vishnu.

10.31

pavanaḥ pavatām asmi rāmaḥ śastrabhṛtām aham |
jhaṣāṇāṁ makaraś cāsmi srotasām asmi jāhnavī ||

Among purifiers, I am the breeze; among wielders of weapons, I am Rama; among aquatic creatures, I am Makara (vehicle of the God of the ocean); among streams, I am Jahnavi (the Ganges).

<u>Explanation:</u>

The analogy is of ***prana,*** is of that which purifies from within. Prana distils life current out of the oxygen we breathe. Pranayama is breath control. Through advanced practice of Pranayama, Yogis achieve this mastery over beath and can sustain themselves on cosmic energy alone.

Amongst wielders of weapons, He is the ideal *uttam purusha* **Rama.** I am *Makara* which is the vehicle of the ocean God Varuna.

The **Ganges River** (Jahnavi) can be likened to the *Sushumna* or life current channel which flows in the spine from the *mooladhar to the sahasrara.* The Ganges represents the ever-flowing intuitive wisdom of a liberated Yogi.

10.32

sargāṇām ādir antaś ca madhyaṁ caivāham Arjuna |
adhyātmavidyā vidyānāṁ vādaḥ pravadatām aham ||

Of all manifestations, O Arjuna, I am the beginning, middle, and end. Among all branches of knowledge, I am the wisdom of the Self, for debaters, I am discriminative logic (vada).

Explanation:

I am **Vishnu Shiva and Brahma**, the preserver or sustainer, the destroyer, and the creator. I am the very discriminating power *(buddhi)* that gives you reason or thirst for knowledge. I am that intuitive intelligence *(chit)*. Man has the power of discriminative logic *(vada)*, abstract reasoning and perception. The correct use of this power allows us to realize the cosmic dream and fathom the cosmic delusion.

10.33

akṣarāṇāṁ akāro 'smi dvandvaḥ sāmāsikasya ca |
aham evākṣayaḥ kālo dhātāhaṁ viśvatomukhaḥ ||

Among all letters, I am the letter A; of all compounds, I am the *dvandva* (connective element). I am Immutable Time; and I am the Omnipresent Creator (the all-pervading Dispenser of Destiny) whose face is turned on all sides.

Explanation:

I am the letter **A**, the start of the cosmic primordial sound **Aum,** which was with Brahman from the beginning, and which can lead you back to me. The start, the connective middle and the Ultimate all knowing all seeing, Am I – the **dvandva**

I am the unchangeable **Time** (eternal consciousness), and I am also the **dispenser of destiny** through the law of good and bad karma. I have 360-degree vision and can see all around, up and down.

10.34

mṛtyuḥ sarvaharaś cāham udbhavaś ca bhaviṣyatām |
kīrtiḥ śrīr vāk ca nārīṇāṁ smṛtir medhā dhṛtiḥ kṣamā ||

I am all-dissolving Death; and I am Birth, the origin of all that will be. Among feminine manifestations (qualities of Prakriti), I am fame, success, the illumining power of speech, memory, discriminative intelligence, the grasping faculty of intuition, and the steadfastness of divine forbearance.

<u>Explanation:</u>

I am **Death and Birth** the origin and finality of all that is, <u>Yama is the Deva of death.</u> Yama means Self Control, the power to guide, restrain and govern oneself.

I am the seven **feminine virtues** of cosmic nature Prakriti. These are namely: <u>Fame, Success, Speech, Memory, Intelligence, Intuition and Calm stability.</u>

These virtues enhance the aspects of our life and are referred to as the 7 Goddesses (*Devi's*)

Cosmic Mother is Shakti and her 7 daughters -

1. **Kirti** Fame or Glory

2. **Shree** Success or Prosperity

3. **Vach** Speech

4. **Smriti** Memory

5. **Medha** Intelligence

6. **Dhriti** Grasping power of intuition

7. **Kshama** Forbearance

10.35

> bṛhatsāma tathā sāmnāṁ gāyatrī chandasām aham |
> māsānāṁ mārgaśīrṣo 'ham ṛtūnāṁ kusumākaraḥ ||

Among Samas (hymns), I am Brihat-Saman, among poetic meters, I am Gayatri; among the months, I am Margasirsha (an auspicious winter month); among seasons, I am Kusumakara, the flower-bearer (Spring).

Explanation:

Amongst the hymns of the Sama Veda, I am the **Brihat Saman**. *Sama* - Means Calm or Tranquil. Acquisition of true knowledge, Realisation of the Ultimate Truth, comes from inner intuitive perception. This is possible only when the mind is tranquil, the yogi concentrates in the agya chakra between his eyebrows, the Kutastha Center of Universal consciousness, and then he becomes a knower of the Vedas, the truth.

Amongst the mantras I am the all-powerful <u>Gayatri Mantra,</u> amongst the months of the year, I am the harvest **margasirsha** month of December / January and amongst the seasons I am the beautifully flowering and alive spring. **(kusumakara)**

In conclusion, it must be said that Krishna is informing Arjuna with seemingly simple examples that everything that he can possibly imagine, everything that he can possibly see and everything that is, is Him!

Here he is extolling his virtues but that does not mean that he is not seen in any negative projections, he is in them too but at this moment of time he does not see the need to explain that aspect of his nature. He does touch on it briefly in the next verse though to keep the balance for Arjuna in case he only looks for Glory...

Symbolically, this is also a message for us to realize the vast extent of our own limitless potential and what we must achieve in our journey to be one in union.

<u>10.36</u>

> dyūtaṁ chalayatām asmi tejas tejasvinām aham |
> jayo 'smi vyavasāyo 'smi satvaṁ satvavatām aham ||

I am the gambling of the practisers of fraud, Of all the deceptive plays, I am the Dice-play.
I am the radiance of the radiant; I am victory and the striving power,
I am the quality of satva amongst the good.

Explanation:

In his verse Krishna is depicting the three qualities of Tamas, Rajas and Satva, inherent in Nature. Krishna is the ever-present Reality in the delusive forces of Nature.

The gambler who courts tamasik qualities, The thinker who chooses to rise above it (Rajasik) and those who favor a life of discrimination and goodness (Satvik), are all part of his cosmic delusion, the great drama that is life!

Those who are born are controlled by maya and the three gunas and dualities of nature. One has to use one's discrimination and free will choice to first understand and then uplift themselves from this play of maya, to become one with Brahman.

10.37

vṛṣṇīnāṁ vāsudevo 'smi pāṇḍavānāṁ dhanaṁjayaḥ |
munīnām apy ahaṁ vyāsaḥ kavīnām uśanā kaviḥ ||

Among the Vrishnis, I am Vasudeva (Krishna); among the Pandavas, I am Dhananjaya (Arjuna); among the munis (saints), I am Vyasa; among the sages, I am the savant, Ushanas.

Explanation:

Sri Krishna is extolling the best of the best.

He was born to Vasudeva who belonged to a tribe called **Vrishnis.** He talks about Himself as **Vasudeva,** an avatar with a physical body to show the identity between Brahman and His manifestations. The only other son of Vasudeva is Balarama. Krishna's glory as the son of Vasudeva is the all-powerful Balarama who is the direct source of all other avatars or incarnations including Rama and Vishnu.

He says He is Arjuna among the **Pandavas,** as Arjuna was the most qualified and it was, he who asked Him for knowledge (*gyana*).

Arjuna is considered the best of the Pandavas. He is also known as Dhananjaya - The Winner of Wealth.

Ved Vyasa, the author of the Mahabharata, the 18 Puranas, Brahma sutras and the one who compiled the 4 Vedas is the most exalted among the *Munis.* Vyasa is the best amongst the **Rishis and Munis.** Vyasa was also the pen name of Krishna Dwaipayan who introduced a revolutionary style of writing philosophies and religious texts. He constitutionalized the Vedas and helped not only in passing but also for preserving knowledge.

Ushanas also called Shukracharya, the priest of the asuras had the power to revive the dead. Krishna declares Himself to be the great poet, **Sage Ushanas.**

10.38

daṇḍo damayatām asmi nītir asmi jigīṣatām |
maunaṁ caivāsmi guhyānāṁ jñānaṁ jñānavatām aham ||

**I am the rod of the discipliners; I am the art of those who seek.
victory: I am also the silence of all hidden things, and the wisdom, of
all knowers.**

Explanation:

The **Rod is symbolic** of the law of cause and effect - Karma, the ultimate discipliner! The Rod is our Spinal Cord which must be held erect in self-discipline during meditation ☐☐ postures. The Rod located in our back, works as the Law of Karma or cause and effect, from which no one can escape.

Brahman's all conquering power is manifested in right actions and noble goals. The karmic law is a science and an Art, that has no parallel! Brahman's silent presence in all of Creation is his best kept secret, discernible by the only the few seekers of this eternal Truth.

10.39

yac cāpi sarvabhūtānāṁ bījaṁ tad aham Arjuna |
na tad asti vinā yat syān mayā bhūtaṁ carācaram ||

**I am, furthermore, whatsoever constitutes the reproductive seed of
all beings. There is nothing, O Arjuna, moving or motionless, that
can abide without Me.**

Explanation:

Ekam Sat - only one truth exists. In the Vedas, the cosmos is said to evolve like a spider's web out of Brahman's being. He is the divine thread or unifying essence running thru all experiences and all expressions of life and matter.

The entire universe is a divine manifestation of Brahman in all its diversities.

The true doctrine of omnipresence is that Brahman appears with all his parts in every moss and cobweb.

In this verse 39, He concludes his list of glories by stating that He is the seed of eternal creation - the cause of all manifestation, therefore whatever form comes forth, one should always think about the consciousness that is pervading that form.

He says there is nothing that is separate from ME.

10.40

nānto 'sti mama divyānāṁ vibhūtīnāṁ paraṁtapa |
eṣa tūddeśataḥ prokto vibhūter vistaro mayā ||

O Scorcher of Foes (Arjuna), limitless are the manifestations of My divine attributes: My concise declaration is a mere intimation of My proliferating glorious powers.

Explanation:

The above examples are a few frail attempts to describe divine glories.

The apparent multiplication of Brahmans is bewildering at first glance. but soon we discover that these are all the same Supreme in different aspects and functions. There is always an uttermost God that defies personification.

10.41

yad yad vibhūtimat satvaṁ śrīmad ūrjitam eva vā |
tat tad evāvagaccha tvaṁ mama tejoṁśasambhavam ||

Any being that is a worker of miracles, that is a possessor of true. prosperity, that is endowed with great prowess, know all such to be manifested sparks of My radiance.

Explanation:

Those who are born are controlled by Maya and the three gunas and dualities of nature. One has to use one's discrimination and free will choice to first understand and then uplift us from this play of maya, to become one with Brahman. Very few have the spiritual maturity and equanimity to realize this.

The six glories given to mankind to experience the world of Maya are:

Wealth, knowledge, beauty, fame, power and success. Getting dependent and trapped by these powers we lose sight of the true initiator which is the Supreme Spirit (Purusha)

10.42

athavā bahunaitena kiṁ jñātena tavārjuna |
viṣṭabhyāham idaṁ kṛtsnam ekāmśena sthito jagat ||

But what need hast thou, O Arjuna, for the manifold details of this wisdom? (Understand simply:) I, the Unchanging and Everlasting, sustain and permeate the entire cosmos with but one fragment of My Being!

Explanation:

He says, Do you really want all these details to achieve wisdom? I sustain and permeate into the entire cosmos and simply understanding this aspect will lead you to me.

Esoteric Explanation:

The Lord is also the Law of Karma, which dispenses justice as per our actions. He is the silent presence in all manifestation hidden by the solid veil of Maya. His best-kept secret and workings of karmic order is the central force of our life on planet earth.

There are no parts of Him, He is always complete, whole. This manifold divisions that we perceive with our mind are due to the blessings of Maya, which for theoretical sake is just a fraction of the Supreme Source and the rest is unavailable for our mind's perception, as it is apparently beyond its normal capacity. There is so much more than our limited human mind can ever perceive!

Even by listening to all these glories, Arjuna does not achieve union. He still has to realize that the fraction-less pervades the entire creation with but a fraction of His Yogic power.

The will of Brahman is for us to enjoy his bliss through many forms, and thus he sends forth his *ananda* as four fundamental creative ideas impinged in three *gunas*:

Vibration	**Aum** [energy and consciousness come together to make creative vibration of aum] it is an **anahat** sound, caused without friction
Time	Kaal
Space	Desha [time and space create a distance between creation and dissolution]
Atom	Anu [the idea of particles for manifestation of form]

Chart 33

<u>Refer to the Glossary 1 at the start of the book and in the Glossary at the end of the book for **chakra** reference</u>

<u>Task 9: Name the eight vasus. What does the word Vasu mean?</u>

Summary of Chapter 10

Vibhuti Yoga

The Infinite Manifestations of The Unmanifest Spirit

This chapter deals with the understanding that the Self or Soul of each being is the ultimate Source. By meditating on the Self, we worship Divinity itself.

Sri Krishna tells Arjuna that he is the complete manifestation of Brahman.

Krishna reveals that since He is the beginning, middle, and end of all things, everything that exists is a manifestation of His powers. He is omnipotent, omniscient and omnipresent.

Brahman's (Sat) essential nature is formless and infinite.

The Universe is created through differentiation of Brahman's consciousness.

The Cosmic intelligences is TAT and the Cosmic energy that creates is Maha Prakriti

The light of Brahman equally pervades all beings and objects.

But those beings of superior quality reflect his manifestations to a greater degree (*Vibhuti*)

Multi divisions of his comics intelligence unite, divide, combine in 'Time and Space' to produce new modulations with name, form, and personality.

Ishvara is present in all manifestations, the good, bad, ugly, or otherwise. Nothing can exist without having its source in consciousness. He is the *jagat karana* - the efficient and material cause. He is the storehouse of all potential and all manifestation/creation is but a fraction of that potential.

In any manifested form [that is not realized], potential is limited. However, some of His potential is shining through us and similarly all manifestations have some glory, and some attributes which have their basis in Brahman.

There is identity [oneness] between the Microcosm and the Macrocosm. The part is never separate from the whole. it is always inherent in the whole. The individual mind is part of the total mind. similarly, the individual gross body [Pinda] is part of the total gross body [Brahmand]. so, the individual and total enjoy a part-whole relationship.

Brahman is the eternal consciousness, unchanging and indivisible, in which the illusions of time [change] and space [division] present an infinite variety of forms interacting in a progressive mode of past, present and future.

There is an underlying oneness underlying the multiplicity! We are the non-dual reality as per the Vedas. Investigate the present reality with awareness and everything appears to awareness!

Once we realize this, it takes away all suffering and brings Bliss. There is no second reality apart from this - *TAT TVAM ASI!*

Those who are born are controlled by Maya and the three Gunas and dualities of nature. One must use one's discrimination and free will choice to first understand and then uplift us from this play of Maya, to become one with Brahman.

Arjuna is also called **Gudakesha**: The esoteric meaning of Gudakesha (Arjuna) is the conqueror of Sleep ⌨- Maya – Ignorance – Delusion. The one who conquers Ignorance, is forever in Knowledge *Jnana* and is Awakened!

He asks - "Should I worship you as Cosmic Consciousness or as having attributes, many aspects and forms" "How will I recognize you in my mind during Meditation"?

It is very difficult for us to imagine nothingness and sink into nothingness, so we have given Brahman a shape / form and focused on an image. This gave rise to Dvait (Duality) - where we looked at Brahman outside of us in another form, full of power, mystery and majesty.

Our existence starts from a point of awareness, perception and looking at the world from within to without. We need to reverse this from without to within. Man is the only living being which has the power of reasoning. He can make choices - this, or that. All other creatures operate on instinctive behavior patterns.

Human Knowledge will always be limited without the wisdom derived from intuitive perception of the Soul. This intuitive perception is the energization of the *Agya Chakra* which imparts true wisdom.

It must be noted here that this speech is meant to be inspirational, it is related to us reaching our very own highest potential. Making us the best version of ourselves. This is the ideal depiction of the cosmos (para prakriti), and HE is therefore inspiring us to reach that pinnacle of excellence that we are naturally endowed to attain.

In every verse the lesson is that there are ordinary men and men of great powers.

These names before us are the examples of ideal depictions of humans…

The following <u>glossary</u> is in reference to all the contextual comparisons in Chapter 10, of the verses 10.6-31

Glossary 2 of Names

No	Names	Terms	Meaning
1	Marichi, Atri, Angiras, Pulaha, Kratu, Pulastya Vashishtha	Great Rishis (7), Maha Rishis, or Deva Rishis	The principal powers of consciousness and life from the creative cosmic energy (Aum)
2	Narada, Asita, Devala, Vyasa, Bhrigu	Great Sages or Divine seers	Preceptor of the Astral devas, liberated in spirit.
3	Sanaka, Sanandana, Sanatana, Sanat Kumara	Primeval Four (4) Ushanas The mind born sons of Brahma	Ancient, Joyful, Everlasting, youthful
4	Svayambhuva, Svarochisha, Auttami, Tamasa, Raivata, Chakshusha, *Vaivasvata**, Savarni, Daksha, Brahma, Dharma, Rudra, Rauchya and Indra Savarni	Manu's (14) Fathers of mankind	*Vivasvat* (7th) is* the progenitor of the present race, only 4 of these Manu's could create the human being
5	Aryama, Dhata, Mitra, Rudra, Varuna, Surya, Bhaga, Vivaswan, Pusa, Savita, Tvasta and Vishnu	Adityas (12) according to linga puranas they are divine, uplifting forces	Bright and pure as streams of water, free from all guile and falsehood, blameless, perfect, upholding Dharma. Protectors of all beings, who guard the world of spirits and protect the world.
6	Ishvara, Hiranyagarbha, Virat, Pragya, Taijas, Vishva	Divine Angels (6)	Creative Intelligence / Forces, Deities who govern the physical, subtle and causal worlds and bodies.
7	The sky, earth, wind, fire stars, water, sun and the moon	Vasus (8)	8 Vitalizing and Intelligent deities of the elements

No	Names	Terms	Meaning
8	Pavaka - The purifying and vitalizing deity	Agni the God of fire	The sacrificial fire that receives and consumes the oblations given in sacrifices
9	Kapali, Pingala, Bhima, Virupaksa, Vilohita, Shastra, Ajapad, Ahirbhudhnya, Shambhu, Chanda, Bhava	Rudras (11) radiant beings	Shankara is the Supreme empowering power of the 11 Rudras
10	Mooladhar, svadhisththan, manipura, anahat, vishudhi, agya, sahasrara	Chakras (7)	7 energy centers, vortices, along the subtle spinal column
11	They are twins with head of a horse but the rest of the body of human beings.	Twin Ashvins (2)	Vedic gods symbolizing the shining of sunrise and sunset.
12	Hanuman is a wind God, a supreme of all Maruts	Maruts (49 wind Gods) riding in golden chariots drawn by ruddy horses.	They are described as armed with golden weapons i.e. lightning and thunderbolts, as having iron teeth and roaring like lions, as residing in the north
13	Rig, Yajur, Sama and Atharva	Vedas (4)	Vedas means knowledge. They are a large body of the oldest scriptures of Hinduism
14	Gandharvas	Celestial Demi Gods	Those who serve as musicians of the devas
15	Chitra ratha	Principal Gandharva	Having a bright chariot depicting the sun
16	Desire; The God of Love,	Kamadeva	The first Awakening of Desire
17	Personified Creative Consciousness.	Kandarpa	God of love, sex, desire for creation.
18	Kubera -The lord of riches and the king of mythical yakshas	Yakshas, Rakshasas	Dishonest, traitorous, greedy, selfish and possessive.

No	Names	Terms	Meaning
19	Ananta, & Shesha Nag, The divine or celestial serpents	Naga serpents	Eternal, that which remains suspended betwixt creation cycles
20	Brihaspati	Chief amongst priests	Deva of evolution or expansion of creation through power of cosmic delusion
21	Skanda, Kartikeyan, son of Shiva	Amongst Generals	God of war, represents self-control that drives away the ego and senses
22	Om or Aum	Sacred Chant	The primordial vibration of Brahman
23	Silent Superconscious Chanting	Yajnas, Japas	Oblation, praise, offerings accompanied by chanting of Vedic mantras
24	Kapila a vedic sage, founder of the Samkhya school of Philosophy	Siddha	as per the puranas, he is an avatar come to earth to restore the spiritual balance through his teachings.
25	Ashvattha Fig / Pipal Tree/ Bodhi	Trees	Has its roots in heavens, and it is a tree of eternal life.
26	Meru - Top of the cerebrum, Sahasrara Chakra	Mountain peaks	Highest place of divine consciousness in the body
27	Aryama - Ancestors, parents	Pitris,	The supreme creative light of the astral world and is the younger brother of the shesha naga who serves Vishnu
28	Sama Veda	Sama Veda	That veda which deals with music & art and is full of calming and tranquilizing hymns for realisation
29	Gayatri Mantra: One of the two classes of sacred verses	Mantra	Holds the essence of the entire Vedas in one Mantra
30	Brihat-Saman: the second of the two classes of sacred verses	Mantras	Name of one of the two chief hymns

No	Names	Terms	Meaning
31	Vasuki The coiled sleeping serpent who adorns the neck of lord Shiva	Kundalini	This is in reference to the creative forces that have their origin in kundalini, the coiled life energy center at the base of the spine that enlivens the senses and uplifts spiritual perceptions.
32	Vasudeva Krishna	Vrishnis /Yadava	Descendant of the Vrishni dynasty of the Yadava race
33	Indra - Demi God	Vasava	Chief of Astral Gods, conqueror of the senses. Wisdom is his vehicle.
34	Airavata	Indra's wild elephant	Elephant is a symbol of wisdom
35	Gita, the Vedas and 108 upanishads	Upanishads (108)	Holy Scriptures
36	A teacher or Guru	Preceptor	Responsible to uphold a certain law or tradition, a precept.
37	Uchchaihshravas the nectar born stallion	Horse of the sun God	Wondrous horse that arose out of the churning of the ocean by the gods and demons who were trying to recover the lost nectar of immortality
38	Kamadhuk	Celestial cow	Fulfiller of all desires,
39	God of death	Yama	
40	God of the ocean	Varuna	
41	Demons and Titans or Giants	Danavas	The mythical demons and giants who fought against the Gods
42	Vehicle of Varuna, the god of ocean	Makara	The mythical sea creature
43	Prahlada	Daitya - demons	Prahlada was a daitya, but he still shunned evil
44	Jahanvi	The Ganges	Maha Prakriti/Consciousness/Chaitanya

No	Names	Terms	Meaning
45	Dvandva	Connective	In Sanskrit, *dvandva* refers to a class of compound words.
46	Vehicle of Vishnu	Garuda	Lord of the skies
47	Margasirsha	Most auspicious and healthiest period of the year	Period spanning winter months of November and December
48	Kusumakara	Time of spiritual fulfillment	A place abounding with flowers. Spring
49	Ushanas	Savant	The ancient sage and poet
50	The Puranas (Sanskrit: पुराण purāṇa, "of ancient times") are Hindu religious texts.		The Hindu Maha Puranas are traditionally attributed to "Vyasa", but many scholars considered them likely the work of many authors over the centuries. The Bhagavata Purana has been among the most celebrated and popular text in the Puranic genre.

Om   Creative Vibration

Tat   Ishvara or Kutastha Chaitanya

Sat   Brahman

BHAGAVAD GITA VOLUME – 2

Chapter 11

Vishva roop darshan Yoga - Vision of Visions

The Lord reveals His Cosmic Self

Introduction to Chapter 11

In the previous chapters, the Supreme Lord Krishna has explained exhaustively, how He is immanent in all of Creation, and all the objects of the world...

Arjuna requests for a demonstration of all that is described to him, and Krishna bestows on him this special grace and honor.

To be able to see the Self in all of reality, one needs to qualify. Spiritual intuition is that special vision which comes accompanied by supreme grace, deep spiritual knowledge and discriminative intelligence.

Therefore, Krishna demonstrates this very theory, that he has been expounding and shows Arjuna his "ultimate form". Visual demonstration is more effective than hearsay.

Arjuna's third eye is energized to help him experience that he is one with him. With grace, the third eye [*ajna* chakra] is opened for the pure of heart and soul, to see the Divine form [Vishwa Roop].

As he beholds the Supreme in everything and everything in the Supreme, he is struck with wonderment, fear, reverence, and devotion.

Note to reader:

Most verses in Chapter 11 must ideally be chanted in sanskrit for the vibratory blessings to stir and awaken within us the memory of Truth and Realisation held deep in the inner sanctum of our Soul (Atman)

This vision of visions is in song metre, and is a homage to the universal form of Spirit (Brahman)

Vishva roop darshan Yoga – Vision of Visions

The Supreme reveals His Cosmic Self

11.1-4

Arjuna uvāca:
madanugrahāya paramaṁ guhyam adhyātmasaṁjñitam |
yat tvayoktaṁ vacas tena moho 'yaṁ vigato mama ||

bhavāpyayau hi bhūtānāṁ śrutau vistaraśo mayā |
tvattaḥ kamalapatrākṣa māhātmyam api cāvyayam ||

evam etad yathāttha tvam ātmānaṁ parameśvara |
draṣṭum icchāmi te rūpam aiśvaraṁ puruṣottama ||

manyase yadi tac chakyaṁ mayā draṣṭum iti prabho |
yogeśvara tato me tvaṁ darśayātmānam avyayam ||

11.1

Arjuna said:

Thou hast compassionately revealed to me the secret wisdom of the true Self, thus banishing my delusion.

11.2

O Lotus-Eyed (Krishna)! Thou hast told me extensively of the beginning and end of all beings, and of Thine eternal sovereignty.

11.3

O Great One! truly hast Thou thus declared Thyself. Yet, O Purushuttama! I long to see Thee in Divine Embodiment (Thine Ishvara - Form).

11.4

O Master, O Supreme of Yogis! if Thou deemest me able to see It, show to me Thine Infinite Self!

Arjuna says, "You have revealed to me thy secret wisdom and banished my delusion.

You have given me an extensive explanation of the beginning and end of all beings and of your eternal reign. Although you have declared all that, yet I long to see this form of yours, I want to experience thee.

I beseech thee to show thyself. I yearn to see your form, if you consider me worthy of such a vision".

Esoteric Explanation:

Seeing has a deeper impact than listening. Although Arjuna is convinced of all that Krishna has described, Arjuna is still full of curiosity. He is not satisfied with just listening about the glories of the Lord and requests him to grant him the divine vision with which to see his vision in all its glory, provided the Lord deems him capable of being able to fathom this illuminating vision.

This knowledge is so sacred that one needs to be deserving to receive it.

11.5-7

Srī Bhagavān uvāca:

paśya me pārtha rūpāṇi śataśo 'tha sahasraśaḥ |
nānāvidhāni divyāni nānāvarṇākṛtīni ca ||

paśyādityān vasūn rudrān aśvinau marutas tathā |
bahūny adṛṣṭapūrvāṇi paśyāścaryāṇi bhārata ||

ihaikasthaṁ jagat kṛtsnaṁ paśyādya sacarācaram |
mama dehe guḍākeśa yac cānyad draṣṭum icchasi ||

The Blessed Lord said:

11.5

Behold, O son of Pritha (Arjuna)! by hundreds and by thousands My divine forms, multi-colored, omnifarious!

11.6

Behold the Adityas, the Vasus, the Rudras, the twin Ashvins, the Maruts, and many wonders hitherto unknown!

11.7

Here and now, O Conqueror of Sleep (Arjuna)! behold as unified in My Cosmic Body all worlds, all that moves or is. motionless, and whatever else thou desirest to see.

Explanation:

Krishna transforms into a divine manifestation in Arjuna's mixed response of awe, love, and fear because he has moved from an intellectual to an experiential understanding of Krishna's teachings with unalloyed devotion and meditation.

11.8

na tu māṁ śakyase draṣṭum anenaiva svacakṣuṣā |
divyaṁ dadāmi te cakṣuḥ paśya me yogam aiśvaram ||

But thou canst not see Me with mortal eyes. Therefore, I give thee. sight divine. Behold My supreme power of yoga!

Explanation:

In normal mortals, our eyes do not see the Divine. Sight divine is bestowed on those who are worthy of His grace. With grace, the third eye is opened for those pure of heart and soul, to see the divine form of Ishvara. Ishvara opens the third eye of the devotee, to make him experience that he is one with him. Here Krishna is explaining to Arjuna, by making him visualize the divine vision of Ishvara.

In this verse, the Agya chakra or energized third eye ◉ is explained as the eye of intuition. Krishna says we all have it, but it needs to be energized, (with Raja Yoga techniques) as it is currently covered in veils of ignorance. It is with this intuitive eye ◉ that faith changes to a direct experience of divinity!

11.9

Sanjaya uvāca:
evam uktvā tato rājan mahāyogeśvaro hariḥ |
darśayām āsa pārthāya paramaṁ rūpam aiśvaram ||

Sanjaya said (to King Dhritrashtra):

With these words Hari (Krishna), the exalted One of Yoga, revealed to Arjuna the consummate embodiment, the Cosmic bodied form.

Explanation:

Lord Krishna shows Arjuna his ultimate form.

He exposes his infinite manifestations, unveiling the Maya exposing his Self. He gives Arjuna divine gaze through his third eye in the forehead, between the eyebrows, and revealed his cosmic bodied form.

Sanjaya has been gifted the boon of divine vision, given to him by Sage Ved Vyasa, Divine sight through introspection.

11.10-14

anekavaktranayanam anekādbhutadarśanam |
anekadivyābharaṇaṁ divyānekodyatāyudham ||

divyamālyāmbaradharaṁ divyagandhānulepanam |
sarvāścaryamayaṁ devam anantaṁ viśvatomukham ||

divi sūryasahasrasya bhaved yugapad utthitā |
yadi bhāḥ sadṛśī sā syād bhāsas tasya mahātmanaḥ ||

tatraikasthaṁ jagat kṛtsnaṁ pravibhaktam anekadhā |
apaśyad devadevasya śarīre pāṇḍavas tadā ||

tataḥ sa vismayāviṣṭo hṛṣṭaromā dhanaṁjayaḥ |
praṇamya śirasā devaṁ kṛtāñjalir abhāṣata ||

11.10-11

Arjuna saw the multifarious marvelous presence of the Deity - infinite in forms, shining in every direction of space, omnipotence - all pervading, adorned with countless celestial robes. and garlands and ornaments, upraising heavenly weapons, fragrant with every lovely essence, His mouths, and eyes everywhere!

11.12

If a thousand suns appeared simultaneously in the sky, the light might dimly resemble the splendor of that Omnific Being!

11.13

There, resting within the infinite form of the Brahma, Arjuna beheld the entire universe with all its diversified. manifestations.

11.14

Then the winner of wealth (Arjuna), wonder-struck, his hair standing on end, his palms together in a prayerful gesture, bowing his head in awe before the Supreme, addressed Him

Explanation:

Arjuna saw the entire Astral and Physical Universe in the shape of a Cosmic Body, evolved as a causal dream of Ishvara.

Ishvara has no form but assumes many forms. When free of delusion, and one with Brahman, we realize that He is beyond physical, astral and causal worlds and yet all of it!

11.15-31

Arjuna uvāca:

paśyāmi devāṁs tava deva dehe sarvāṁs tathā bhūtaviśeṣasaṁghān |
brahmāṇam īśaṁ kamalāsanastham ṛṣīṁś ca sarvān uragāṁś ca divyān ||

anekabāhūdaravaktranetram paśyāmi tvāṁ sarvato 'nantarūpam |
nāntaṁ na madhyaṁ na punas tavādiṁ paśyāmi viśveśvara viśvarūpa ||

kirīṭinaṁ gadinaṁ cakriṇaṁ ca tejorāśiṁ sarvato dīptimantam |
paśyāmi tvāṁ durnirīkṣyaṁ samantād dīptānalārkadyutim aprameyam ||

tvam akṣaraṁ paramaṁ veditavyaṁ tvam asya viśvasya paraṁ
nidhānam |
tvam avyayaḥ śāśvatadharmagoptā sanātanas tvaṁ puruṣo mato me ||

anādimadhyāntam anantavīryam anantabāhuṁ śaśisūryanetram |
paśyāmi tvāṁ dīptahutāśavaktraṁ svatejasā viśvam idaṁ tapantam ||

dyāvāpṛthivyor idam antaraṁ hi vyāptaṁ tvayaikena diśaś ca sarvāḥ |
dṛṣṭvā 'dbhutaṁ rūpam ugraṁ tavedaṁ lokatrayaṁ pravyathitaṁ
mahātman ||

amī hi tvāṁ surasaṁghā viśanti kecid bhītāḥ prāñjalayo gṛṇanti |
svastīty uktvā maharṣi siddhasaṁghāḥ stuvanti tvāṁ stutibhiḥ
puṣkalābhiḥ ||

rudrādityā vasavo ye ca sādhyā viśve 'śvinau marutaś coṣmapāś ca |
gandharvaya kṣāsura siddha sangha vīkṣante tvāṁ vismitāś caiva sarve ||

rūpaṁ mahat te bahuvaktranetram mahābāho bahubāhūrupādam |
bahūdaraṁ bahudaṁṣṭrākarālaṁ dṛṣṭvā lokāḥ pravyathitās tathāham ||

nabhaḥspṛśaṁ dīptam anekavarṇaṁ vyāttānanaṁ dīptaviśālanetram |
dṛṣṭvā hi tvam pravyathitāntarātmā dhṛtiṁ na vindāmi śamaṁ ca viṣṇo ||

daṁṣṭrākarālāni ca te mukhāni dṛṣṭvaiva kālānalasaṁnibhāni |
diśo na jāne na labhe ca śarma prasīda deveśa jagannivāsa ||

amī ca tvāṁ dhṛtarāṣṭrasya putrāḥ sarve sahaivāvanipālasaṁghaiḥ |
bhīṣmo droṇaḥ sūtaputras tathāsau sahāsmadīyair api yodhamukhyaiḥ ||

vaktrāṇi te tvaramāṇā viśanti daṁṣṭrākarālāni bhayānakāni |
kecid vilagnā daśanāntareṣu saṁdṛśyante cūrṇitair uttamāṅgaiḥ ||

yathā nadīnāṁ bahavo 'mbuvegāḥ samudram evābhimukhā dravanti |
tathā tavāmī naralokavīrā viśanti vaktrāṇy abhivijvalanti ||

yathā pradīptaṁ jvalanaṁ pataṅgā viśanti nāśāya samṛddhavegāḥ |
tathaiva nāśāya viśanti lokās tavāpi vaktrāṇi samṛddhavegāḥ ||

lelihyase grasamānaḥ samantāl lokān samagrān vadanair jvaladbhiḥ |
tejobhir āpūrya jagat samagraṁ bhāsas tavogrāḥ pratapanti viṣṇo ||

ākhyāhi me ko bhavān ugrarūpo namo 'stu te devavara prasīda |
vijñātum icchāmi bhavantam ādyaṁ na hi prajānāmi tava pravṛttim ||

Arjuna said:

11.15

Beloved Supreme, Adored of all Gods! Behold, Thy body holds. All fleshly tenants, seers fine, And diverse angel-Brahmans divine.

Dwelling deep in mystery cave, The serpent nature's forceful crave, Though fierce and subtle, now is tame, forgetful of her deadly game.

And Sovran Brahma, Brahman of Brahmans, On lotus seat is snug secured.

11.16

Great Cosmic-Bodied Supreme of worlds, Oh, I behold, again behold.

Thee all and everywhere, Thy countless arms, trunks, mouths, and eyes! Yet drooping, dark, my knowledge lies. About Thy birth and reign and ending here.

11.17

This day, O Blazing, Furious Flame, O Blinding Ray, Thy focused power's aglow: Thy Name Spreads everywhere To dark'st abysmal lair.

Gilded with a crown of stars. And wielding mace of sovereign power, Thou whirlest forth, O Burning Phoebus, Thine evolution's circling discus.

11.18

Immortal Brahma, all Supreme, Thou Cosmic Shelter, Wisdom's Theme, Eternal Dharma's Guardian true, Thou diest not I ever knew!

11.19

O Birthless, Fleshless, Deathless One, I see Thine endless, working arms, Thine ever watching eyes of suns and moons, the staring skies.

And from Thy mouth spumes throbbing flame, As utterest Thou the Aum, Thy Cosmic Name.

Thy Self-born luster shields from harm, And all creation, distance-flung, doth warm.

11.20

O Sovereign Soul! 'Twixt earth and home of Brahmans, Directions all, and earthly sods, All high abodes and all encircling spheres,

By Thee pervaded, far and near. The worlds-triune awestruck by fear, Thy dreadful wondrous form adore.

11.21

In Thee the Brahmans their entry makes with folded hands, afraid, some pray to shelter take. In Thee.

The seers great, and heaven's-path successful ones, With superb chants of "Peace!" do worship Thee and Thee alone.

11.22

Th' eleven lamps of heaven. The twelve bright suns. The grizzly eight, The starry lusters great.

Aspiring hermits; patron Brahmans, The agents of the cosmic Lords.

The twin-born princes strong, Of valor known so long. Two-score and nine noil breezes' force, That binds the atom close.

The long-passed guardian spirits all. The demi goblins, demigods, and demons tall.

And mighty ones in Spirit's path, In wonder gaze upon Thy blazoned worth.

11.23

I Thee behold, colossal-armed! With starry eyes and countless cheeks,

With endless hands, and legs adorned with lotus feet. Thy chasmed mouth with doomsday's teeth Doth yawn to swallow swooning worlds above, beneath,

And leaves a distilled joyous awe in me: Thy grandeur I and all are wonder struck to see!

11.24

To view the bowels of the void deep all filled with Thee, Thy gaping mouth and diverse hues of fiery lustrous body-

O Vishnu of the flaming sight, Thou quite o'erpowerest me, my peace dost fright.

11.25

Ferocious teeth and deadly fires do howl. In mouths of Thine that at me scowl. Directions four are lost and gone, Compassion show! I find no peace alone.

O Cosmic Guardian, Brahmans, Be pleased t'accept my humble pleading words.

The sons of senses swayed with kingly pride, With ego, karmic habit, worldly lure, abide. And wait to leap upon our wisdom's chiefs, And yet they all do ride. The race of death, to fall and hide.

11.26

Fore'er in Thy devouring mouth, Adorned with crushing cruel teeth uncouth. The victor and the vanquished must (Thine offspring both, the righteous and ungodly ones)

Thy love still claims; yet all someday shall kiss the dust, And sleep on common floor of earth. The shattered skulls of some are seen, As caught Thy greedy teeth between.

11.27

As diverse, restless, watery waves Of river branches all do crave To force through crowded wavelets' way And meet where Neptune's home long lay,

E'en so, heroic streams of life Do plunge to meet in maddest strife. Within Thy foaming mouth of flaming sea, Where sparks of lives all dance in Thee.

11.28

As insects lost in beauty's game. All swiftly, thoughtless, rush to flame, So, fog-born passion's fires pretend. To glow like heavenly light of Thine and draw on mortals to attend. The trumpet call to deathly line.

11.29

Thy mouth ablaze doth bring to gaze. Its leaping tongues to lick. The angry blood of strong and weak.

11.30

Thou, gourmand Brahman, dost eat. With hunger infinite. O Vishnu, Thou dost scorch The worlds with all-pervading fiery torch.

11.31

Be pleased, O First of Brahmans. I ache to know, Primeval Supreme, True who Thou art-O Fiery Mood, Yet so benign and good. Oh, tell me Thy Royal Will. For it I know not still.

11.32-34

Srī Bhagavān uvāca:

kālo 'smi lokakṣayakṛt pravṛddho lokān samāhartum iha pravṛttaḥ |
ṛte 'pi tvāṁ na bhaviṣyanti sarve ye 'vasthitāḥ pratyanīkeṣu yodhāḥ ||

tasmāt tvam uttiṣṭha yaśo labhasva jitvā śatrūn bhuṅkṣva rājyaṁ samṛddham |
mayaivaite nihatāḥ pūrvam eva nimittamātraṁ bhava savyasācin ||

droṇaṁ ca bhīṣmaṁ ca jayadrathaṁ ca karṇaṁ tathānyān api yodhavīrān |
mayā hatāṁs tvaṁ jahi mā vyathiṣṭhā yudhyasva jetāsi raṇe sapatnān||

The Blessed Supreme Lord then said:

11.32

In guise of endless doom, I come as avaricious time to seize and room.

In burning maw of mine the weaklings' awe, and all the mortal meat of weary worlds of deathly change and treat.
Them with My nectar-life To new and fearless, better strife.

E'en if thou dost forbear to slay.

Thy wicked foes, still they-and warriors all in brave array will sure and certain timely have to fall, Ah, in My righteous teeth-of-law, withal.

11.33

Arise, awake! Arise, awake! Dash thou upon the foe, the flesh a captive makes.

And win the victor's fame. With battle-hunted game. Wealth of the King Of peace, and heaven's kingdom, bring! I know right now the happenings all.

That mystic future forth doth call. And thus, thy foes and warriors true, Long, long ago I slew,

Ere shalt thine agent-hand (That I would wield to land Thy foes on death's dim shore). Now understand!

11.34

My agent thou. Oh, this is how. I work My plans-the universe-

Through instruments diverse. Tis I who slew and yet will slay the senses' train

Through thee, as through both past and future ones, My soldiers sane!

Explanation: **11.32-34**

The purpose of human creation is to evolve spiritually into our worthy and ideal manifestations and then to work on neutralizing our individual karmic storehouse.

Yes, it's up to us to have complete acceptance and surrender to the divine so that life can become a worthy tribute to Him.

He created the dualities of raga dvesha etc., to experience the cosmic drama as a witness, to enjoy but also, HE warned us to not get attached to Maya

Once we become the Lord's partner, all conflicts will disappear!

11.35-42

Sanjaya uvāca:

etac chrutvā vacanaṁ keśavasya kṛtāñjalir vepamānaḥ kirīṭī |
namaskṛtvā bhūya evāha kṛṣṇaṁ sagadgadaṁ bhītabhītaḥpraṇamya || (35)

Arjuna uvāca:

sthāne hṛṣīkeśa tava prakīrtyā jagat prahṛṣyaty anurajyate ca |
rakṣāṁsi bhītāni diśo dravanti sarve namasyanti ca siddhasaṁghāḥ || (36)

kasmāc ca te na nameran mahātman garīyase brahmaṇo 'py ādikartre |
ananta deveśa jagannivāsa tvam akṣaraṁ sad asat tatparaṁ yat || (37)

tvam ādidevaḥ puruṣaḥ purāṇas tvam asya viśvasya paraṁ Nidhānam |
vettāsi vedyaṁ ca paraṁ ca dhāma tvayā tataṁ viśvam anantarūpa || (38)

vāyur yamo 'gnir varuṇaḥ śaśāṅkaḥ prajāpatis tvaṁ prapitāmahaś ca |
namo namas te 'stu sahasrakṛtvaḥ punaś ca bhūyo 'pi namo namas te || (39)

namaḥ purastād atha pṛṣṭhatas te namo 'stu te sarvata eva sarva |
anantavīryāmitavikramas tvaṁ sarvaṁ samāpnoṣi tato 'si sarvaḥ || (40)

sakhe 'ti matvā prasabhaṁ yad uktaṁ he kṛṣṇa he yādava he sakheti |
ajānatā mahimānaṁ tavedaṁ mayā pramādāt praṇayena vāpi || (41)

yac cāvahāsārtham asatkṛto 'si vihāraśayyāsanabhojaneṣu |
eko 'thavāpy acyuta tatsamakṣaṁ tat kṣāmaye tvām aham aprameyam || (42)

Sanjaya said (to King Dhritarashtra):

11.35

After hearing the words of Keshava (the maya-transcendent Krishna),
the diademed one (Arjuna, haloed with cosmic vision), trembling and
awestricken, joining his palms in worshipful supplication, again, made
humble obeisance and addressed Krishna in a quavering voice:

Arjuna said:

11.36

O Hrishikesha (Krishna)! rightly are the worlds proud and gladdened
to exude thy glory! the demons, terrified, seek safety. in distance, while
the multitudes of siddhas (perfected beings) bow down to worship
thee.

11.37

and why should they not pay thee homage, o vast spirit? for greater
art thou than brahma the creator, who issued from thee. o infinite
one, o Brahman of Brahmans, o shelter of the universe, thou art the
imperishable-the manifested, the unmanifested, and that beyond (the
ultimate mystery).

11.38

the primal Purusha art thou! the pristine spirit, the final refuge of
the worlds, the knower and the known, the supreme fulfilment! thine
omnipresence shines in the universe, o thou of inexhaustible form!

11.39

O flowing life of cosmic currents (vayu), o king of death (Yama), O Lord of flames (agni), O sovereign of sea and sky (Varun), O Supreme of night (the moon), O divine father of countless offspring (Prajapati), O ancestor of all! to thee praise, praise without end! to thee my salutations thousandfold!

11.40

O endless might, o invincible omniscient omnipresence, o all-in-all! I bow to thee in front and behind, I bow to thee on the left and the right, I bow to thee above and beneath, I bow to thee. enclosing me everywhere!

11.41

unaware of this, thy cosmic glory, and thinking of thee as a familiar companion, often have I audaciously hailed thee as "friend" and "Krishna" and "Yadav." for all such words, whether spoken carelessly or with affection.

11.42

and for any irreverence I have displayed toward thee, o unshakable Lord! in light-hearted mood at mealtimes or while walking or sitting or resting, alone with thee or in others' company-for all such unintentional slights, o thou illimitable! I beg forgiveness.

11.36-42

Explanation:

This is when Krishna reveals his true self ...

This vision of visions is in song metre, and is a homage to the universal form of Spirit (Brahman)

These verses must ideally be chanted in sanskrit for the vibratory blessings to stir and awaken within us the memory of Truth and Realisation held deep in the inner sanctum of our Soul (Atman)

Arjuna realizes the vastness of Brahman - the imperishable, the eternal infinite, the ever present, unbound, unrelated to time and space. He is trembling and fearful. His kundalini shakti has whipped up and he is in an ecstatic state as well as transformational yogic state of third eye visualization.

11.43

Arjuna said:

pitāsi lokasya carācarasya tvam asya pūjyaś ca gurur garīyān |
na tvatsamo 'sty abhyadhikaḥ kuto 'nyo lokatraye 'py
apratimaprabhāva ||

Arjuna says:

Father of All art Thou! of animate and inanimate alike. None but There
is worthy of worship, O Guru Sublime! Unparalleled by any other
in the three worlds, who may surpass Thee, O Supreme of Power
Incomparable?

Explanation:

Now Arjuna supplicates himself in front of the Krishna, in awe and in his praise. He alone who is selfless, free from malice, jealousy, pride and ego may be able to receive this, Grace.

11.44-55

Arjuna uvāca:

11.44

tasmāt praṇamya praṇidhāya kāyam prasādaye tvām aham īśam īḍyam |
piteva putrasya sakheva sakhyuḥ priyaḥ priyāyārhasi deva soḍhum ||

Therefore, O Adorable One, I cast myself in obeisance at Thy feet to implore Thy pardon. As a father to his son, as a friend to a close friend, as a lover to his beloved, do Thou, O Supreme, forgive me!

11.45

adṛṣṭapūrvam hṛṣito 'smi dṛṣṭvā bhayena ca pravyathitam mano me |
tad eva me darśaya deva rūpam prasīda deveśa jagannivāsa ||

Overjoyed am I at having gazed upon a vision never seen, before, yet my mind is not free from terror. Be merciful to me, O Brahman, O Shelter of the Worlds! Show to me only Thy Deva form. (as the benign Vishnu).

11.46

kirīṭinam gadinam cakrahastam icchāmi tvām draṣṭum aham tathaiva |
tenaiva rūpeṇa caturbhujena sahasrabāho bhava viśvamūrte ||

I long to see Thee as before, as the four-armed Vishnu, diademed and holding Thy mace and discus. Reappear in that. same form, O Thou who art thousand armed and universe bodied!

Explanation:

Arjuna begs forgiveness from the Krishna for doubting him. He says although I am overjoyed yet I am in terror. Do not show me evil but only the divine forms.

Please re appear as Vishnu or as my friend Krishna for I am unable to look at you in this giant form.

11.47-49

Srībhagavān uvāca:

mayā prasannena tavārjunedam rūpam param darśitam ātmayogāt |
tejomayam viśvam anantam ādyam yan me tvadanyena na dṛṣṭapūrvam || (47)

na vedayajñādhyayanair na dānair na ca kriyābhir na tapobhir ugraiḥ |
evaṁrūpaḥ śakya ahaṁ nṛloke draṣṭuṁ tvadanyena kurupravīra || (48)

mā te vyathā mā ca vimūḍhabhāvo dṛṣṭvā rūpaṁ ghoram īdṛṅ mamedam |
vyapetabhīḥ prītamanāḥ punas tvaṁ tad eva me rūpam idaṁ prapaśya || (49)

11.47

I have graciously exercised Mine own yoga power to reveal to thee,
O Arjuna, and to none other! This supreme primeval form of Mine,
the radiant and infinite Cosmos!

11.48

No mortal man, save only thyself, O great hero of the Kurus! can
look upon my universal shape-not by sacrifices or charity or
works or rigorous austerity or study of the Vedas is that vision
attainable.

11.49

Be not affrighted or stupefied at seeing My terrible aspect, with
dreads removed and heart rejoicing, behold once more My familiar
form!

Sanjaya said (to King Dhritarashtra):

11.50

Sanjaya uvāca:

ity Arjunaṁ vāsudevas tathoktvā svakaṁ rūpaṁ darśayām āsa bhūyaḥ |
āśvāsayām āsa ca bhītam enaṁ bhūtvā punaḥ saumyavapur mahātmā ||

After speaking thus, Vasudeva, "the lord of the World," resumed his own
shape as Krishna. He, the Great-Souled One, appearing to Arjuna in the
form of grace, consoled His fear stricken. devotee.

11.51

Arjuna uvāca:

dṛṣṭvedaṁ mānuṣaṁ rūpaṁ tava saumyaṁ janārdana |
idānīm asmi saṁvṛttaḥ sacetāḥ prakṛtiṁ gataḥ ||

O Granter of All Wishes (Krishna)! As I gaze on Thee again in gentle human shape, my mind is quieted, and I feel more like me, me natural self.

11.52-54

Srī Bhagavān uvāca:

sudurdarśam idaṁ rūpaṁ dṛṣṭavān asi yan mama |
devā apy asya rūpasya nityaṁ darśanakāṅkṣiṇaḥ || (52)

nāhaṁ vedair na tapasā na dānena na cejyayā |
śakya evaṁvidho draṣṭuṁ dṛṣṭavān asi māṁ yathā || (53)

bhaktyā tvananyayā śakya aham evaṁvidho 'rjuna |
jñātuṁ draṣṭuṁ ca tattvena praveṣṭuṁ ca paraṁtapa || (54)

11.52-54

Sri Krishna replies:

But it is not unveiled through one's penance or scriptural. lore or gift giving or formal worship.

O Scorcher of the Sense Foes (Arjuna)!

only by undivided devotion (commingling by yoga all thoughts in One Divine Perception)

may I be seen as thou hast beheld Me in My Cosmic Form and recognized and finally embraced in Oneness!

The Blessed almighty said:

**Very difficult it is to behold, as thou hast done, the Vision Universal!
Even the Devas ever yearn to see it.**

Through my yogic power, I have revealed myself to you.

11.55

matkarmakṛn matparamo madbhaktaḥ saṅgavarjitaḥ |
nirvairaḥ sarvabhūteṣu yaḥ sa mām eti pāṇḍava ||

**He who works for Me alone, who makes Me his goal, who lovingly
considers Me the Supreme, who is non-attached (to My delusive
cosmic-dream worlds), who bears ill will toward none, (beholding
Me in all) he enters My being, O Arjuna!**

Explanation:

So far Arjuna had looked upon Krishna as his friend and cousin. He had not known of the glories of the lord in its entirety.

He had behaved with Krishna as he would an ordinary person, laughing and joking and debating. Now after being graced with the special vision of visions, he sees and recognizes and stands in awe of the Lord in all his diverse forms, magnanimous and over-powering, scary in its magnitude.

He then prays that Krishna comes back to him in his gentler form, the form he is familiar with. He needs no more convincing.

He feels within himself, the tremendous power of the exploding 1000 suns or 1000 petalled lotus at the Sahasrara Chakra. This is the path of Self-Realisation.

He sees the magnificence of the Omnipresent, Omniscient and Omnipotent Ishvara and along with him, Sanjaya, who stands for introspection also sees this magnificent illusion.

Task 10 for reader: How did Arjuna visualize the Supreme Source as revealed to him?

Summary of Chapter 11

Sri Krishna reveals His cosmic Self as Ishvara

Arjuna saw Creation, Preservation and Dissolution continuously rolling in to the light of the Spirit.

Awakening of realisation to the cosmic play happens for Arjun.

As he beholds the Supreme in everything and everything in the Him, he is struck with wonderment, fear, reverence, and devotion. Lord Krishna's transformation into a divine manifestation, results in Arjuna's mixed response of awe, love and fear because he has moved from an intellectual to an experiential understanding of Krishna's teachings through unalloyed devotion.

Lord Krishna shows Arjuna his ultimate form. He teaches selflessness, freedom from malice, jealousy, pride and ego. He reveals his infinite manifestations, unveiling Maya and exposing His Super Self. The Supreme has no form but assumes many forms.

When free of delusion, and one with Brahman, we realize that he is beyond physical, astral, and causal worlds and yet all of it!

We live in an amazing world, made even more wonderful with science and technology. At any given time in this world, there is everything and nothing, best and worst. Outstanding feats are happening around us but what we perceive, and experience depends on our attitude and mental state of being.

The Lord gives us divine eyes... we only need to change our disposition! We see the world as we want to see it. It is up to us to qualify to see the best, the highest, the ultimate.

Brahman has created dualities in Creation, for us to experience his cosmic drama. We are to enjoy every experience but never to get attached. He remains as the witness.

When free of delusion and in Union, Arjuna realizes that he is beyond physical, astral, and causal worlds and yet all of it.

What makes the difference? Our attitude and our mind. What is needed is to change the thought patterns in our mind. We can be miserable at the best of times with negative attitude, and we can be deliriously happy at the worst of times with positive attitude. There is no place for grief in our lives.

Bhagavad Gita helps us to rein in negative thoughts, refine the mind with positive thoughts and finally, to eliminate the influence of the mind.

Bhagavad Gita inspires with a higher ideal saturated with universal love. It satisfies with knowledge therefore helps to relieve suffering due to ignorance, and problems are taken care of.

How does one grow and evolve? *Tasmat Tvam Uthishtha [thus you Rise]*

Engage with our demons, understand our faults. identify our endowments, explore possibilities.

<u>7 usual states of a human</u>

1. Couch Potato – indolent, lazy - Tamasik

2. Materialist - Rajasik and Tamasik

3. Sensualist - Rajasik and Tamasik

4. Power Hungry - Rajasik

5. Sentimental - Rajasik and Tamasik

6. Cerebral - Satvik and Rajasik

7. Spiritual – Satvik

Moha (attachment) is entanglement, and the passion that holds us back, that restricts and limits our abilities and brings us only misery. When there is no *shraddha,* no trust, what dawns is *moha* - a feverishness, and fear of losing that which we are attached to.

We need to change our perception from petty, mundane & trivial to a lofty, inspired sense of living.

It is our own mind which is the enemy; because of delusion and moha (attachment), we see what we want to see! The mind projects imaginary problems, torments us, and itself suffers the most in the end. Being the Divine's partner will result in all conflicts disappearing.

Om Creative Vibration

Tat Ishvara or Kutastha Chaitanya

Sat Brahman

BHAGAVAD GITA VOLUME – 2

Chapter 12

Bhakti Yoga - Union Through Devotion

Introduction to Chapter 12

In this Chapter Lord Krishna gives detailed explanation of who is a true devotee, his qualities, and the different ways that people adopt to worship him.

Apara bhakti, Para bhakti, Sagun Bhakti, Nirgun Bhakti are all differentiated. Ultimately, a true devotee is one who with total surrender and devotion leads his life selflessly, without getting attached to the fruit of his action, for the higher purpose of attaining the best for others, the highest within himself and becoming one with Brahman.

This is the 6th and final chapter on Bhakti Yoga.

This chapter stresses on the super-excellence of the path of loving devotion over all other types of spiritual practices.

In this chapter Arjuna asks Krishna, which is the higher form of Bhakti?

Bhakti towards a God with form or towards an unmanifested Brahman – *Sagun Bhakti or Nirgun Bhakti.*

Bhakti Yoga – Union Through Devotion

12.1

Arjuna uvāca:

evaṁ satatayuktā ye bhaktās tvāṁ paryupāsate |
ye cāpy akṣaram avyaktaṁ teṣāṁ ke yogavittamāḥ ||

Arjuna said:

Those devotees who, ever steadfast, thus worship Thee; and those who adore the Indestructible, the Unmanifested-which of these is better versed in yoga?

Explanation:

Here Arjuna starts by asking who is a better yogi One who treads the path of Bhakti Yoga or Jnana Yoga? Also, which is better- praying to the Unmanifested Brahman or the Manifested Ishvara?

Arjuna now wants to know, who is a better yogi-the one who follows the path of devotion, looking upon Brahman as the supreme person, with a form [Sakar], or the one who looks upon him as the impersonal absolute, with no form [Nirakar].

12.2

Srī Bhagavān uvāca:

mayy āveśya mano ye māṁ nityayuktā upāsate |
śraddhayā parayopetās te me yuktatamā matāḥ ||

The Blessed Supreme said:

Those who, fixing their minds on Me, adore Me, ever united to Me with supreme devotion, are in My eyes the perfect knowers of yoga.

Explanation:

Krishna says both are dear to him, but the scientific practice of Bhakti Yoga is much quicker and easier for personal evolution.

What is this Union through Bhakti?

For average men and women, the concept of Brahman has to be of one with a form, a sort of superior being in human form on whom one can fix one's mind, esp. during prayer. Worshipping a form becomes easier initially...*Sagun bhakti.*

In *Sakar Bhakti Yoga* the devotee chooses a form of the *Saguna Brahman* or Ishvara in any of his manifestations and realizes Him through love and devotion.

Intense faith in a personal deity, called the *Ishta-Deva,* is characteristic of bhakti worship.

Worshiping Him in a personal manifestation and being One with that manifestation, one realizes Him in which ever form and manner that we seek.

This is in Duality when we seek "him" outside of us. This tradition is called" Dvait".

These verses also speak of the Advait philosophy of Nirgun Bhakti where Brahman is without attributes, without form or shape or any kind of containment.

12.3-4

ye tvakṣaram anirdeśyam avyaktaṁ paryupāsate |
sarvatragam acintyaṁ ca kūṭastham acalaṁ dhruvam ||

saṁniyamyendriyagrāmaṁ sarvatra samabuddhayaḥ |
te prāpnuvanti mām eva sarvabhūtahite ratāḥ ||

But those who adore the Indestructible, the Indescribable, the Unmanifested, the All-Pervading, the Incomprehensible, the Immutable, the Unmoving, the Ever Constant, who have subjugated all the senses, possess even mindedness in every.

circumstance, and devote themselves to the good of all beings- verily, they too attain Me.

<u>Explanation:</u>

12.3 - 4 In Bhakti Yoga, we do get all the success and benefits of this world. Transcendence from the sense joys of this world is only achieved through the elixir of divine Samadhi states.

Unmanifested - *Nirgun Brahman* The formless infinite.

Manifested - Idols in homes and temples or Avatars – e.g. Lakshmi, Rama, Shiva and Krishna etc.

When in Advait, he sees divinity of the supreme source in all of creation.

1. No difference between caste, creed, sex, religion etc.

2. Applies various prescribed methods of focus and concentration.

3. Detaches his ego from senses.

4. Attaches his life force, ego, mind to the super conscious soul.

5. Experiences the Kutastha Intelligence in all creatures through Nirvikalpa samadhi and attains the Spirit beyond phenomena.

12.5

> kleśo 'dhikataras teṣām avyaktāsaktacetasām |
> avyaktā hi gatir duḥkhaṁ dehavadbhir avāpyate ||

> **Those whose goal is the Unmanifested increase their difficulties, arduous is the path to the Absolute for embodied beings.**

<u>Explanation:</u>

The issue here is that human mind cannot comprehend the formless infinite, so it is easier to worship Brahman with a form and hence we transfer this Bhakti to an image that we know - the human body.

This is the Dvait tradition - Idol worship. Worship of a deity/idol outside of us and transferring all the reverence to this idol beyond the self becomes easier. Bhakti is often a deeply emotional devotion based on a relationship between a devotee and the object of devotion.

The *Ishta Deva* can be one of the trinities, anyone of the avatars or any deity of one's choice.

In the first stage of Bhakti Yoga, the form of the *Ishta Deva* is visualized by means of an image or icon. It is installed in the home and pooja performed daily - *Apara Bhakti.*

It must be understood that the image installed is not considered Brahman but a symbol of godhead, in order to get the devotee to concentrate his mind totally on Brahman.

According to Ramana Maharishi, bhakti is a surrender to divine vibration with one's heart. It can be practiced as an adjunct to self-inquiry in one of the four ways:

Atman - Bhakti	Devotion to the Supreme Self
Ishvara - Bhakti	Devotion to Ishvara with form or formless.
Ishta Deva - Bhakti	Devotion to a personal God or Goddess
Guru - Bhakti	Devotion to one's Guru.

12.6-7

ye tu sarvāṇi karmāṇi mayi saṁnyasya matparāḥ |
ananyenaiva yogena māṁ dhyāyanta upāsate ||

teṣām ahaṁ samuddhartā mṛtyusaṁsārasāgarāt |
bhavāmi na cirāt pārtha mayy āveśitacetasām ||

**But those who venerate Me, giving over all activities to Me.
(thinking of Me as the Sole Doer), contemplating Me by single
minded Yoga remaining thus absorbed in Me - indeed,**

**O offspring of Pritha (Arjuna), for these whose consciousness is
fixed in Me, I become before long their Redeemer to bring them out
of the sea of mortal births.**

Explanation:

Those who are in total surrender and non-doer ship and are in Samadhi state, get Moksha. They need not come back to play again on this earthly plane. The heart converts into complete acceptance of worldly life as a tribute to creation.

Here something very interesting is stated: we breathe approximately 21,000 times in one day.

With each breath we can evolve, yogis do exactly that, they use each breath to commune with the divine; we can too!

We must use our breath, the space between breaths, to Realize the Self, be in self-realisation and become one with Spirit. That is the purpose of our entire being 🙏

12.8

mayy eva mana ādhatsva mayi buddhiṁ niveśaya |
nivasiṣyasi mayy eva ata ūrdhvaṁ na saṁśayaḥ ||

Immerse thy mind in Me alone; concentrate on Me thy discriminative perception; and beyond doubt thou shalt dwell immortally in Me.

Explanation:

These are all various ways to achieve Self-realisation. This verse is the summary of all the above verses, simplified.

1. Renunciation of fruits of action, keep performing spiritually strong actions and do not focus on the outcome, be in the journey with only one destination, that of self-realisation.

2. With *viveka,* we develop wisdom, the intuitional spiritual knowledge when put into practice is referred to as *Viveka.* It is the power to discriminate between right and wrong, truth and untruth.

3. Intellect is theoretical, but Meditation gets us intuitional knowledge.

4. Peace comes from non-attachment.

5. Meditation has many states and Yogis spend lifetimes progressing to higher stages of meditational bliss. *Savikalpa and Nirvikalpa Samadhi* are types of samadhi.

6. But maybe, we should not worry about the stages of samadhi yet, as our current role is to progress by *Antahakaran Shuddhi* (inner purification) to achieve a *Stith Pragya* (Undisturbed) state of peace.

12.9

atha cittaṁ samādhātuṁ na śaknoṣi mayi sthiram |
abhyāsayogena tato mām icchāptuṁ dhanaṁjaya ||

O Dhananjaya (Arjuna), if thou art not able to keep thy mind wholly on Me, then seek to attain Me by repeated yoga practice.

Explanation:

Sri Krishna advises even the most restless of devotees, the one who lacks the karmic disposition that facilitates yoga practice is to meditate persistently anyway for the love of Brahman, and a desire to please him. with this continuous spiritual practice, he will ultimately succeed in self-realisation.

Even the most restless of devotees, who due to karmic preconditions cannot sit still, may out of divine love and continual spiritual activity, be able to attain Self-realisation.

Nine obstacles on the spiritual path of a yogi are:

1.	**Vyadhi** illness of body
2.	**Styana** illness of the mind
3.	**Sanchay** doubt
4.	**Pramada** carelessness, negligence, carelessness, casual attitude
5.	**Alasya** laziness in abhyas, practice
6.	**Brahnti Darshan** delusion hallucinations misguided
7.	**Alabadh bhumikatva** inability to hold what has been achieved
8.	**Avivritti** - inabilities to let go of cravings
9.	**Anavastitattva** - inabilities to maintain continued progress

Chart 34

One pointedness on OM is needed to overcome the above, this is a repetitive practice and can become boring and cause restlessness, but is necessary for everlasting peace, clarity, joy, as does a familiar experience, the known, bring peace.

The ultimate state of bliss is Ishvara, it is eternal, cannot die. Consciousness has no limitations. It cannot change and cannot die.

12.10

abhyāse 'pyasamartho 'si matkarmaparamo bhava |
madartham api karmāṇi kurvan siddhim avāpsyasi ||

If, again, thou art not able to practice continuous yoga, be thou diligent in performing actions in the thought of Me. Even by engaging in activities on My behalf thou shalt attain supreme. divine success.

Explanation:

We are born with certain tendencies and Gunas. All are not able to follow the path of Bhakti Yoga. For the restless, for those who are not able to concentrate on Yogic practices, the path of Karma-Yoga is suggested. Self-less actions dedicated with loving surrender to Brahman, ensure the same results.

12.11

athaitad apy aśakto 'si kartuṁ madyogam āśritaḥ |
sarvakarmaphalatyāgaṁ tataḥ kuru yatātmavān ||

If thou art not able to do even this, then, remaining attached to Me. as thy Shelter, relinquish the fruits of all actions while continuing. to strive for Self-mastery.

Explanation:

Bhakti or devotion in its ultimate form binds the devotee to Brahman without any restrictions of class, color or creed. Nor does it accept any rules of worship.

Atmanivedan and Sharanagati, total surrender to Brahman, is the highest form of Bhakti. Selfless service to others without any attachment to the fruits of action, dis-attachment and Devotion with self- Discipline and self-control are the keys to self-realisation.

12.12

śreyo hi jñānam abhyāsāj jñānād dhyānaṁ viśiṣyate |
dhyānāt karmaphalatyāgas tyāgāc chāntir anantaram ||

Verily, wisdom (born from yoga practice) is superior to (mechanical) yoga practice; meditation is more desirable than the possession of (theoretical) wisdom; the relinquishment of the fruits of actions is better than (the initial states of) meditation. Renunciation of the fruits of actions is followed immediately by peace.

<u>Explanation:</u>

In verses 12.8-12 Krishna urges Arjuna, the seeker, to try for communion (tune into divine vibration) in whichever manner he can. Nothing is written in stone; all paths lead to the same goal of Freedom.

The goal is one, that of Divine Realisation and freedom from being bound within the body.

Here, Krishna gives us a variety of ways to achieve the goal of Self-realisation.

Krishna says to Arjuna (the seeker in all of us) to:

12.8 – practice sitting still and silently in a state of concentration.

12.9 - For the most restless of devotees who due to karmic preconditions cannot sit still, practice the Yogic techniques of Raja Yoga and Kriya yoga science.

12.10 - If we cannot even do that, then ensure to continually practice Spiritual Activity.

Engage the self in works that are devoted to Him and are pleasing to Brahman.

With bhakti, divine love and continual spiritual activity we may be able to attain Self-realisation through selfless service to others.

12.11- if we cannot even not even this, then at least surrender all your activity unto Me (by removing the aham/ego from yourself) abandon the fruits of all works to Brahman.

Such abandonment is very potent; for it can bring peace instantly.

The four paths of Yoga encouraged by Krishna are:

Raj Yog – practice of Meditation techniques of Patanjali's Ashtanga Yoga or Kriya Yoga to attain Samadhi.

Karma Yog – Path of Selfless Service – Relinquishing the fruit of action.

Bhakti Yog – Path of Devotional Service to the Supreme.

Gyana Yog – Pursuit of Spiritual Knowledge

12.13-14

advesṭā sarvabhūtānāṁ maitraḥ karuṇa eva ca |
nirmamo nirahaṁkāraḥ samaduḥkhasukhaḥ kṣamī ||

saṁtuṣṭaḥ satataṁ yogī yatātmā dṛḍhaniścayaḥ |
mayy arpitamanobuddhir yo madbhaktaḥ sa me priyaḥ ||

**He who is free from hatred toward all creatures, is friendly
and kind to all, is devoid of the consciousness of "I-ness" and
possessiveness; is even minded in suffering and joy, forgiving, ever.**

**contented; a regular yoga practitioner, constantly trying by
yoga to know the Self and to unite with Spirit, possessed of firm.
determination, with mind and discrimination surrendered to Me he
is My devotee, dear to Me.**

Explanation:

In these 2 verses are listed 17 spiritual traits that arise when our individual *ahamkara* or ego is annihilated and that is at the core of understanding the teachings of *Bhakti*. The following are qualities that a true devotee aspires for:

Adveshta:	without any dislike, the one who is devoid of hatred, and whose mind and intelligence is engaged in thinking of the Supreme Source, that person is a devotee and is thus very dear to Brahman.
Bhakta:	My Devotee who is only depending on Brahman and nobody else. अन अन्येन योगेन - भक्ति। The devotee who is in total surrender to the Creator for protection as he considers himself to be powerless and dependent, can offer himself to the Supreme.
Ishvara Aashrit:	ईशवर आश्रित । He Depends only on Brahman and none other. He can only love with total devotion and thus Brahman's kindness equips the devotee with all the qualifications. Without Supreme grace no human can attain those qualifications required for Union.
Maitraha:	the one who is friendly and compassionate to all living beings.
Karunaha:	the one who is compassionate.
Nirmamaha:	the one he who is without the sense of ownership, one who is devoid of any sense of possessiveness.
Nirahankaaraha:	the one without egoism and free of egotism.
Sama:	the one who is equipoised forgiving, self-controlled and of strong determination.
Sama dukh sukh:	is same in sorrow and joy objective in all circumstances.
Kshama:	is forgiving.
Santushtha:	is contented.
Satatam:	is a steady practitioner of yoga.
Yog:	is united in devotion.
Yata atman:	is self-controlled.
Dridh anishchayaha:	has firm conviction.
Arpita:	the one who's Mind and Intellect is dedicated to me as an offering - ईश्वरअर्पि।
Manobuddhihi:	is the one who has a dedicated mind and an energized intellect.

<u>Chart 35</u>

12.15

yasmān nodvijate loko lokān nodvijate ca yaḥ |
harṣāmarṣabhayodvegair mukto yaḥ sa ca me priyaḥ ||

A person who does not disturb the world and who cannot be disturbed by the world, who is free from exultation, jealousy, apprehension, and worry, he too is dear to Me.

Explanation:

One who knows that worldly joy and sorrow is a temporary game. He is undisturbed by all the goings on and does not disturb the world either.

12.16

anapekṣaḥ śucir dakṣa udāsīno gatavyathaḥ |
sarvārambhaparityāgī yo madbhaktaḥ sa me priyaḥ ||

He who is free from worldly expectations, who is pure in body and mind, who is ever ready to work, who remains unconcerned with and unafflicted by circumstances, who has forsaken all ego-initiated desireful undertakings-he is My devotee, dear to Me.

Explanation:

Free from Worldly expectations of modern trappings of so-called success, monetary gains, car, house, status, material possessions. He works hard at only one thing - spiritual understanding and upliftment.

12.17

yo na hṛṣyati na dveṣṭi na śocati na kāṅkṣati |
śubhāśubhaparityāgī bhaktimān yaḥ sa me priyaḥ ||

He who feels neither rejoicing nor loathing toward the glad nor the sad (aspects of phenomenal life), who is free from grief and cravings, who has banished the relative consciousness of good and evil, and who is intently devout-he is dear to Me.

Explanation:

Remains unaffected by all kinds of situations in Life; Glad vs Sad, Grief and Cravings (Avoids hankering after temporary thrills).

He has risen above the duality of good and evil and is devoted to Self-Realisation. He understands that duality is part of everything in nature, just as a coin cannot be without two sides.

12.18-19

> samaḥ śatrau ca mitre ca tathā mānāpamānayoḥ |
> śītoṣṇasukhaduḥkheṣu samaḥ saṅgavivarjitaḥ ||
>
> tulyanindāstutir maunī saṁtuṣṭo yena kenacit |
> aniketaḥ sthiramatir bhaktimān me priyo naraḥ ||

He who is tranquil before friend and foe alike, and in encountering adoration and insult, and during the experiences of warmth and chill and of pleasure and suffering,

who has relinquished attachment, regarding blame and praise in the same light, who is quiet and easily contented, not attached to domesticity, and of calm disposition and devotional-that person is. dear to Me.

Explanation:

One who is unaffected by criticism or praise or how others regard him.

In our daily householder's life, the above verses must be given attention and understood properly as we are all caught up with these dualities and emotions.

Deep Introspection and Contemplation is required for understanding creation in relation to the Self. Regular and daily introspection helps us to observe our own shortfalls and correct them.

12.20

> ye tu dharmyāmṛtam idaṁ yathoktaṁ paryupāsate |
> śraddhadhānā matparamā bhaktās te 'tīva me priyāḥ ||

But those who adoringly pursue this undying religion (dharma) as heretofore declared, saturated with devotion, supremely engrossed in Me-such devotees are extremely dear to Me.

<u>Explanation:</u>

"Knowing the Absolute!" defines who the 'Absolute' is and how one can rise to merge with the Supreme Spirit.

He emphasizes here the nectar like qualities that a sincere devotee has. Humility, forgiveness and love of divinity are these virtues. Devotion should be expressed not only by rituals but also by thoughts, actions and emotions.

Bhakti transcends both rituals and intellectual pursuits.

HE concludes by saying that devotion combined by a loving heart, unwavering faith, and selfless action is the most accessible and preferred path. Ultimately it is not merely outer actions but the inner purity of intent and dedication to knowing the Lord, that makes us attain Union.

Bhakti when added to these actions becomes:

Food / *Anna*	⟶	Offering / *Prasad*
Water / *Pani*	⟶	Holy water for purification / *Jal*
Song / *Sangeet*	⟶	Ode / *Kirtan*
Human / *Manav*	⟶	Humanity / *Manavta*
Home / *Ghar*	⟶	Temple / *Mandir*
Heart / *Hridaya*	⟶	Meditation / *Dhyana*
Travel / *Tirtha*	⟶	Pilgrimage / *Tirtha-yatra*
Action / *Karma*	⟶	Charity & Care for others without ego / *Seva-Karma yoga*

<u>Chart 36</u>

<u>Task 11 for the reader: What is the secret path to align with the divine vibration of the cosmos?</u>

<u>Task 12 for reader: What is the importance of a Guru? Who is a preceptor as per Vēdānta?</u>

<u>Summary of Chapter 12</u>

Bhakti Yoga – Union through devotion

Arjuna asks -Which devotee is better?

One who prays to the *Cosmic bodied God* Or the *Formless unmanifested Spirit*?

For average men and women, the concept of the Supreme is usually with a form, a sort of superior being in human form on whom one can fix one's mind, esp. during prayer. Worshipping a form becomes easier initially...*Sagun bhakti.*

In Bhakti Yog the devotee chooses a form of the Sagun Brahman or Ishvara in any of his manifestations and realizes the Self through love and devotion.

Intense faith in a personal deity, called the Ishta-Deva, is characteristic of Bhakti worship.

The *Ishta-Deva* can be one of the Trinity, Brahma, Vishnu, Mahesh; anyone of the avatars or any deity of one's choice.

In the first stage of Bhakti yoga, the form of the Ishta-Deva is visualized by means of an image or icon. it is installed in the home and pooja performed daily. This is called *Apara Bhakti.*

It must be understood that the image installed is considered a symbol of Godhead, to get the devotee to concentrate his mind totally on the divine Spirit.

The 33 koti Devi-Devas described in the Vedas, is wrongly translated as 33 crores whereas the word koti means kinds of Devi-Devas. They are phenomenal beings in the Astral world with the power of gratifying our desires. Praying to the *Devas* and performing rituals bring limited fructification. not eternal liberation and glory.

Worshiping Him in a personal manifestation and being One with that manifestation, understanding the qualities of a true seeker, one realizes Him in which ever form and manner that we seek [Dvait].

In Para Bhakti, the devotee focuses on the Nirgun [formless] Brahman himself. He asks for nothing in return for himself and continues to love the Divine. Such bhakti elevates the devotee, until, in our final stages, we becomes one with divinity [Advait].

The Bhagavad Gita advises even the most restless devotee – the one who lacks the karmic disposition that facilitates yoga practice, to remain persistent in his devotion and with this continuous spiritual practice, he may ultimately succeed in self-realisation.

Bhakti or devotion in its ultimate form binds the devotee to Brahman without any restrictions of class, color, or creed. Nor does it insist on any rules of worship. It is the beauty of Sanatana Dharma that it gives us the freedom to choose a form conducive to our tendencies, with the knowledge that there is only One *Ishvara!*

Ritualistic practices help to inculcate discipline and are preparatory in order to train the mind but without total devotion, reap limited results.

Wisdom [born from knowledge of yoga] is superior to [mechanical] yoga practice; Meditation is more desirable than the possession of theoretical knowledge; The relinquishing of the fruits of action is better than [initial stages] meditation.

One who is devoid of hatred, who is friendly and compassionate to all living beings, who is devoid of any sense of possessiveness, free of egotism, objective in all circumstances, forgiving, a self-satisfied practitioner of yoga, self-controlled, of strong determination, and whose mind and intelligence is engaged in thinking of Brahman – that person is the devotee and is thus very dear to Brahman.

<u>What is this Union through Bhakti?</u>

Worshiping Him in a personal manifestation and being One with that manifestation, understanding the qualities of a true seeker one realizes Him in which ever form and manner that we seek.

BHAGAVAD GITA VOLUME – 2

TAT - Summary of Chapters 7-12

Bhakti Yoga & Surrender

In **TVAM** – the first six chapters of the Bhagavad Gita, we searched who and what am I. These next six chapters of **TAT** are devoted to understanding Brahman and Bhakti Yoga.

We begin by understanding the difference between Spirit and Matter; the *Jivatman* and *Paramatman*; The Temporary versus the Permanent; the Real versus the Unreal and Truth versus the Untruth.

Brahman is that permanent entity, that field of unlimited potential, which is unmanifest, unborn, never dies, always IS, unchanging and Causeless. It is SAT, CHIT, ANAND. It is beyond the capacity of the limited knowing mind to understand Brahman in its entirety!

The Vedas give us this knowledge of Brahman.

That aspect of Brahman which causes the manifestation of the universe, is ISHVAR. Also called Purushottam, Paramatman, Kutastha Chaitanya. This power of *Ishvara* to create, is Maya. Ishvara using the power of Maya created Brahma, Vishnu, Mahesh. This power of Maya allows us to see Many from One, just like the white light that passing thru a prism emerges as many colors as possible—an Illusion.

Brahman, the intelligent cause of the Universe is necessary for Creation. Maya alone cannot do anything, cannot exist without Ishvara.

Sanatana Dharma recognizes that it is easier for us to identify with forms, and hence both worshipping the Lord with a form *Sakar*, and without a form, *nirakar*, are allowed.

The Devis and Devas are presiding deities of phenomenal forces for the gratification of our desires, so that we can ultimately rise above the desires and seek ultimate union with Brahman. The forms of the Devis and Devas were revealed to the Rishis and exist as per the Vedas. They are highly evolved and elevated yonis.

We can focus our devotion on a form we like to attain single-pointed devotion. Ishta-Deva or Kul-deva is a way to keep the family together and enable passing on the traditions to children.

The deities are decorated and venerated with flowers, fruits, colors and smells in order to engage all our five senses.

The mind – manas wanders and the intellect questions. The mind, the intellect and the chitta needs to be reined in with regular practice.

Various practices like *Kirtan, Japas*, mantras help to bring about equanimity. *Shraddha* is keeping the mind open to what is beyond the knowing mind and adoring it.

Bhakti requires various steps of preparation. In bhakti we need to direct our mind, intellect and consciousness towards divinity. Regular practice helps us to overcome these faculties. Ritualistic practices help us to achieve the discipline required.

The human mind sometimes questions the existence of God! It wants proof of Brahman. If we do not believe in Gods existence, we need to question our very own existence!

Is a miracle a chance happening or is it by divine cosmic design? Is it a coincidence or is it meant to happen? Vedanta says nothing occurs by mere chance. The workings of the Universe are in alignment in accordance with a cosmic plan, cosmic design and cosmic intelligence.

Continuously reflecting, contemplating and engaging one's total being in understanding the purpose and goal of human existence can be done by comprehending the precise significance of various verses and conceptions in the Vedic scriptures.

When aligning the self to Divine Union we ask, "Who is Krishna?" "Who is Brahman?"

"Who is the SELF?" "Who is the self?" "Who am I?"

This 'Me' is the divine Krishna or Lord Vishnu speaking as Brahman and it is to be noted that chapters 7-12 speak, describe, and elaborate on Brahman, the Supreme Source.

Practical applications

- **We can choose to make a change by keeping our curiosity and focus alive**

- **Where our focus goes, there energy flows**

- **Training of the mind with will power and self-discipline**

- **Elevate the frequency of our energy**

- **Find a practice to always keep us in the current moment i.e. Pranayama.**

Discriminative Intellect – Buddhi is making the right action choices, leading to ideal & objective prioritizations of the actions we take in Life	
From Ignorance to ⟶	Knowledge & Light
From Worry to ⟶	Self-Awareness, Calmness
From Anxiety to ⟶	Stress free / Wellbeing
From Fear to ⟶	Faith / Surrender /Courage
From Doubt to ⟶	Curiosity / Interest / Passion
From Disinterest to ⟶	Interest / Engagement / Awareness
From Disease to ⟶	Wellness / Health / Well being
From Disintegration to ⟶	Expansion / Largesse
from Exclusivity & Groupism to ⟶	Inclusivity & The feeling of the world is One *Vasudeva Kutumbakam*

States of Spiritual evolution	
An individual goes through 7 stages of spiritual evolution. We may be at any of the following stages in this life. These stages continue to our next life. Spiritual evolvement is a conscious choice we need to make.	
Vivek is Discrimination between *Nitya* (Permanent) and *Anitya* (Temporary) Stages.	
Pamar	when we are at our most indulgent, with wisdom eclipsed. Purpose of our life is pleasure from objects without displaying any sense of discipline, concern, restraint or introspection. We are self-centered and only happy with acquiring objects and playing with these objects.
Vishayi	when one has reached a stage of not want to hurt anyone in his goals for acquisition of goods. But here also the goal for pleasure seeking remains the same. Drive is in seeking happiness from acquiring material objects and services.
Jigyasu	when we start questioning and seeking answers on life and death. There comes a shift in the orientation of choices. We have now started searching for permanent outcomes as satisfaction for the above is saturated and Buddhi are awakened.
Sadhak	his goals are to know the Self, he is not pleasure oriented and is no more in search of a life accentuated by sense satisfaction.
Shishya	when he finds a Guru and surrenders for seeking knowledge and submits to discipline.
Mumukshu	when his goal is for realisation and he desires only that and has an intense desire for freedom, he is the one who stays in the world and lives in it and yet remains a sincere seeker.
Siddha	Self-realized. when he realizes Brahman.

Chart 37

We must rise from *Pamar* to *Siddha*, and this is dependent on our conviction to reach our ultimate goal.

The significance and importance of Gurus

The full moon day of Guru Purnima is dedicated to the guru-preceptors, the masters of humanity. In India it is a very special celebration to offer love, regards, gratitude, honor, and homage to the lineage of master's from whom we learn and continue to do so till the present day.

In the guru tradition of Vedic culture, we have human, non-human, and even elemental gurus from whom we can learn.

Our learning begins in the mother's womb and ends with Realisation. The first guru of our life is the mother, and the ultimate guru is Brahman.

Learning requires no specific age or other conditions. For learning there is no reason or season. It is a natural tendency to expand our lives by expanding our learning. Learning is an attitude. When we open our minds to learning, we continue to learn and evolve at every moment.

Om   Creative Vibration

Tat   Ishvara or Kutastha Chaitanya

Sat   Brahman

In the **Srimad Bhagavatam** - Book Eleven, King Yadu and Sage Avadhuta (a naked monk), converse on the topic of the **Guru–preceptor.**

Here the **Sage Datta Treya** described his twenty-four gurus in *Prakriti* - Nature:

1	Earth	Forbearance & steadfastness	Duty and service to others
2	Wind	Unchanged & unattached	Truth
3	Sky	No boundaries	Self
4	Water	Transparence	Without Pride
5	Fire	Purification	Consumes sin
6	Moon	Waxes and Wanes	Unchanged detachment in the midst of change
7	Sun	Reflection	Of the Greater Self
8	Pigeons	Attachment	Limit attachment
9	Python	Desires	Limit desires
10	Bumblebee	Material benefits	Live gently without being a burden
11	Beekeeper	Hoarding wealth	For a thief's pocket
12	Hawk	Collecting possessions	Are trouble
13	Ocean	Limitless, Timeless & Lucid	The inner self is undisturbed (as the oceans deepest waters are undisturbed)
14	Moth	Senses have many pitfalls	Stay away from the lure of the senses or we burn
15	Elephant	Lust	Enslaves
16	Deer	Fear	Gets trapped by fear
17	Fish	Greed	
18	Prostitute	Repentance	Creates change for the better
19	Child	Innocence	Bliss
20	Maiden	Company is a distraction	Screen out the company of the outside world
21	Snake	Avoidance of company	Solitude
22	Arrowsmith - Archer	Total Focus	Is required to achieve Self-Realisation
23	Spider (his web)	Exuding Creation	Consuming Creation
24	Caterpillar	When we set the mind	That we become

Chart 38

ॐ असतो मा सद्गमय ।
तमसो मा ज्योतिर्गमय ॥

मृत्योर्मा अमृतं गमय ।
ॐ शान्तिः शान्तिः शान्तिः ॥

Om Asato Maa Sad-Gamaya |
Tamaso Maa Jyotir-Gamaya ||

Mrtyor-Maa Amrtam Gamaya |
Om Shaantih Shaantih Shaantih ||

O lord
From the phenomenal world of unreality,
lead me towards the reality of the eternal self,

From the darkness of ignorance,
lead me towards the light of spiritual knowledge,

From the world of mortality and of material attachment,
lead me to immortality...

Sanskrit Glossary 3

A			
abhasa	reflection	*abhichara prayogam*	Black magic
abhijna	direct perception	*abhimana*	pride
abhisheka	pouring water, etc. over any sacred image	*abhyasa*	practice
abhyasi	one who practices	*achala*	unmoving; a hill or a mountain
achamana	sipping water before or after a religious ceremony	*achit*	not sentient
adhara	support	*adhishtana*	substratum
adhyaropa	superimposition	*adhyasika*	superimposed
adyatmika sakti	spiritual power of the self	*adhridha*	weak, not firm
advaita	non-duality	*agami (agami karma)*	actions expected to bear fruit in future births
aham	I	*aham Brahmasmi*	I am Brahman
ahankara	I' sense; the ego-self	*ahimsa*	non-violence
ajatavada	the theory of *advaita* which denies creation	*ajnana*	ignorance
ajna	direction; injunction	*ajnani*	the ignorant, one who has not realized the Self

akara	form or shape	*akasa*	ether; space
akasavani	voice coming from the sky	*akhanda*	undivided
akhandakara vritti	unbroken experience	*akritopasaka*	one who has not done *upasana* or meditation
amrita	immortal	*amrita Nadi*	the name of a yogic nerve
anadi	without beginning	*anahata*	name of a yogic *chakra*
ananda	bliss	*anandamaya kosa*	the sheath of bliss
anandatmann	Self in the state of bliss	*ananta*	infinite; endless
anatmann	non-Self	*anava*	limitation
anichcha	involuntary	*anitya*	transitory
annamaya kosa	sheath of gross matter	*antah (antar)*	internal
antah karanam	the inner organ; the mind	*antah pranayama*	internal breath-regulation
antardhana	disappearance from sight	*antarmukhi manas*	inward-turned mind
anu	atom	*ap*	water
apana	the life-force which goes down	*Apara*	the lower
Apara vibhuti	inferior *vibhuti*	*aparoksha*	direct; immediate
apavada	removal	*ardra*	a star in the constellation of Orion
aruna	red	*arupa*	formless
asamsakti	non-attachment; one of the seven stages of enlightenment	*asana*	sitting posture; seat
asat	not real	*asesha sakshi*	witness of all

asrama	stage of life; a place where hermits and sages live	*asthira*	unsteady
asukavi	one who can verify spontaneously	*asura*	demon
atiasrama (*atyasrama*)	Above the four stages of life	*ati jagrat*	beyond waking
ati sunya	beyond the void	*atita*	beyond
ativahika sarira	the subtle body which remains when the physical body perishes, and which carries the individual to other worlds	*atman* (*n*)	Self
atman Jnani	one who has realized the Self	*atman Nadi*	the name of a yogic nerve
atman nishta	abiding in the Self	*atmannusandhana*	thinking constantly of the Self
atman vichara	enquiry into the Self	*atyanta vairagyam*	total dispassion
avarana	covering	*avarta*	eddy
avastha traya	the three states of consciousness, namely waking, dream and sleep	*avatar*	incarnation of Brahman
avidya	nascence; ignorance	*avritta chakshus*	introverted look
ayatana	repository		
B			
bahir pranayamam	external breath regulation	*bahir mukhi manas*	outward going mind

bahudaka	a *sannyasin* who wanders about	*bahya*	external
bala	child	*bandha*	bondage
bandha hetu	cause of bondage	*beeja*	seed
bhajana	singing Brahman's praises especially in chorus	*bhakta*	devotee
bhakti	devotion	*bhakti marga*	path of devotion
bhashyakara	commentator	*bhavana*	idea
bhoga	enjoyment	*bhoga hetu*	cause of enjoyment
bhogyam	that which is enjoyed	*bhoga vastu*	object of enjoyment
bhokta	enjoyer	*bhuma*	all-comprehensive; the Absolute
bindu	a term used in *Tantrism*	*brahmachari*	a celibate; a student
brahmahatya	the sin of killing a *brahmin*	*Brahmaivaham*	'Brahmans am I'
Brahmajnana	knowledge (realisation) of Brahman	*Brahmajnani*	one who has realized the Self
Brahman	The Supreme Being; the Absolute	*Brahmanishta*	one who is established in Brahman
brahmacharya	celibacy	*brahmakaravritti*	concept in the form of Brahman
Brahmavid	one who has realized Brahman	*Brahma-vid-vara*	one who is a superior among knowers of Brahman
Brahma-vid-varishta	the very best among the knowers of Brahman	*Brahma-vid-varya*	the best among the Knowers of Brahman
Buddha	one who is aware	*buddhi*	intellect
C			
Chaitanya	Consciousness	*chakshus*	eye

chamara	a fly whisk made of the bushy tail of *Bos grunniens* used as a badge of royalty	*chanchala*	changing, fickle
chidvyoman (*chitta vyoman*)	expanse of consciousness	*chinmaya*	full of Consciousness
chinta	thought or idea	*chintamani*	wish-fulfilling gem
chit	Consciousness	*chitta*	memory; mind
chitta-nirodha	control of mind	*chitta suddhi*	purity of mind
chitta vilasa	play of mind	*chittaikograta*	one-pointedness of mind
D			
daharakasa	ether of the heart	*dana*	gift
darsan(a)	seeing; vision	*dasi*	courtesan
deha(m)	body	*dehatman buddhi*	I-am-the-body consciousness
dehavasana	attachment to the body	*devas*	celestial beings
dharana	concentration of mind; one of the eight stages of *Raja Yoga*	*dharma sastri*	one who is well-versed in the scriptures relating to *dharma*
dhriti	steadfastness	*dhyana*	meditation; contemplation
dikpalas	Brahmans who protect the various quarters	*diksha*	spiritual instruction
divya chakshus	divine eye	*drashta*	seer
dridha	firm	*drik*	he who sees; the subject
drishti	look	*drishti srishti*	simultaneous creation
drisya	that which is seen; the object	*drisyanuviddha*	associated with something seen
drisya vilaya	the disappearance of the objective world	*dukkha*	misery; frustration

dvaita	Duality pair of opposites	*dvandva*	connectives
dvividha (*dwividha*)	two-fold		
E			
eka	one	*ekagrata*	concentration
G			
ganja	a narcotic, *hashish*	*Gayatri*	a well-known Vedic *mantra*
gopuram	temple tower	*granthi*	knot
grihastha	householder	*grihini*	housewife
gunas	the three fundamental qualities, tendencies or stresses which underlie all manifestations	*gunatita*	one who has transcended the *gunas*
guru	a spiritual master; teacher		
H			
halahala	the poison which came up when the milky ocean was churned	*hamsa*	a *sannyasi* who has advanced to a high stage
hasta	hand	*hatha yoga*	a form of yoga involving bodily postures
hetu	cause	*Hiranyagarbha*	universal consciousness; totality of minds
homa	sacrifice in fire	*hridaya*	heart; the spiritual center in the body
hridaya granthi	knot of the heart	*hrit*	heart
hrit pundarika	the heart lotus		

I			
ichcha	desire	*idam*	this
indriyas	senses	*ishta devata*	the Brahman whom one likes to worship or contemplate
Ishvara	Brahman, the Supreme Being in His aspect as all of Creation	*Ishvara anugraha*	Brahman's grace
Ishvara aradhana	worship of Brahman	*Ishvara drishti*	Seeing everything as Brahman
lsvara prasada	Brahman's grace		
J			
jada	inert	*jagat*	world
jagrat	waking state	*jagrat sushupti*	wakeful sleep
jai	victory	*jala*	water
janma	birth	*japa*	repetition of a sacred word or syllable or a name of Brahman
japa karta	one who does *japa*	*jirna*	decayed
Jiva	the individual soul; the ego	*jivanmukta*	one who is liberated even when he is alive
jivanmukti	liberation while one is alive	*jivatmann*	the individual self
jnana(m)	knowledge	*jnana bhumikas*	stages of knowledge of which there are seven
jnana chakshus	eye of wisdom	*jnana drishti*	eye of wisdom
jnanagni	fire of wisdom	*jnana lakshana*	sign of wisdom
jnana marga	the path of knowledge	*jnana yoga*	the method of realizing the Absolute through knowledge
jnanendriya	organ of knowledge	*Jnani*	the Self-realized sage

Jyoti	(*Jyoti*) light; effulgence		
K			
kaivalya	the state of liberation	*kala*	a term used in Tantrism
kalpana	Idea	*kama*	desire; lust
kantha	throat	*kanthabharana*	ornament worn round the neck
kanya	virgin	*karana*	cause
karana sarira	causal body	*karma*	action; work; deeds; also result of action
karma samya	good and bad actions in equal proportions	*karma traya*	the three kinds of karma, namely *sanchita, agami* and *prarabdha*
karma yoga	the spiritual path of action	*karmendriya*	organ of action
karpura arati	the waving of lighted camphor during *puja*	*karta*	he who does an act
kartrtva	doer ship	*kartrtva buddhi*	the sense of doer ship
kashaya	latent impurity	*kashaya*	ochre colored garment
kasiyatra	pilgrimage to Kasi; part of the marriage rites among Brahmins	*kasturi*	musk
kayakalpa	a medicinal preparation for prolonging life	*kayasiddhi*	making the body proof against injury
kevala kumbhaka	sudden stoppage of breathing, whether during inhaling or exhaling	*kevala samadhi*	*samadhi* in which activities of body and mind are merged
khanda	division	*Krama mukti*	liberation by degrees
krama srishti	gradual creation	*kshetra*	temple; field; the body
kshipta	active	*khyati*	theory

kousalam	skill	*krida*	play, pastime
kritopasaka	one who has done *upasana* or meditation	*krodha*	anger
kumbha	a pot used for keeping water	*kumbhaka*	retention of breath
kundalini	yogic power called the serpent power	*Kumkuma*	vermilion powder applied to the forehead
kutichaka	a *sannyasin* who lives permanently in a hut	*kuvasana*	Negative tendencies
L			
laghu	light; easy	*lakshana*	sign
lakshya	aim, target, goal	*lakshyartha*	implied meaning
laya	dissolution	*lila* (*leela*)	play or sport
linga	symbol	*Linga sarira*	subtle body
Loka	world: that which is seen	*loukika*	worldly
M			
madhya	center; mixed; middling	*madhyama*	a stage of uttering sounds
maharshi	great *rishi* (seer or sage)	*mahasunya*	great void
mahatman	enlightened person	*mahavakyas*	the four main sentences proclaiming the truth of Brahman, one taken from each Veda
malaparipaka	complete removal of impurity	*malina*	impure
manana	thinking over what has been heard	*mani*	jewel
manolaya	(temporary) subsidence of the mind	*Mano maya kosa*	sheath of mind
manonasa	extinction of the mind	*manta*	thinker

Mantra also seed (beej) letters for meditation on the form of the Supreme;	Cosmic sound forms of the Vedas used for worship and prayer; ritual, incantation	*mantra japa*	repetition of a *mantra*
marga	path	*maru marichika*	mirage seen in a desert
mati	thinking power	*maya*	illusion: the power inherent in Brahman by which it manifests the world
maya vada	the doctrine of *maya*	*medha*	intellect
Moda	joy which is higher than priya	*moksha*	Liberation; spiritual freedom
moodha	dull	*moola*	root; source
mooladhara	One of the yogic centers of the body	*mouna* (*mowna*)	Silence
mriga trishna	water of mirage	*mukta*	one who is liberated
mukti	Liberation; spiritual freedom	*Mulavidya*	primal ignorance
mumukshu	one who aspires for Liberation	*mumukshutva*	the desire for Liberation
muni	sage	*muppazh*	three voids
N			
na medhaya	not by the intellect	*nada*	subtle sound accompanied by an effulgence; a term used in Tantrism
nabhi	navel	*nadaswaram*	the pipe of the South Indian piper
Nadi	yogic nerve	*naham*	I am not
naishtika brahmacharya	lifelong celibacy	*nama*	name; the name of Brahman

nama japa	repetition of the name of Brahman	*nama sankirtan*	Singing the names of Brahman
nama smarana	remembering and repeating the name of Brahman	*namaskar (a:)*	prostration before Brahman or Guru
nana	diversity	*naraka*	hell
nasa	destruction	*nava*	new
nididhyasana	the last of the three stages of vedantic realisation; uninterrupted contemplation	*nijananda*	true bliss
nirakara upasana	meditation on the formless	*nirguna*	without attributes
nirguna upasana	meditation on the attribute less Brahman	*nirodha*	control
nirvana	Liberation	*nirvikalpa samadhi*	the highest state of concentration in which the soul loses all sense of being different from the universal Self, but a temporary state from which there is a return to ego-consciousness
nishkama karma	acts done without a motive	*nitya*	always, eternal
nitya siddha	ever present	*nivritti*	destruction
nivritti marga	The path of renunciation	*niyama*	
O			
owpacharika	in a worldly sense		
P			
padarthabhavini	absolute non-perception of objects; one of the seven stages of enlightenment	*panchakshari*	a *mantra* of five syllables sacred to Siva

panchikarana	division of the five elements and combining the parts in particular proportion	*para*	higher; in Tantrism unmanifest sound
param	transcendental	*paramahamsa*	a *sannyasin* who has attained Self-realisation
paramarthika	absolute	*paramarthika satyam*	absolute reality
paramatman (*n*)	the Supreme Self	*paranchi khani*	outgoing
para-Nadi	the name of a yogic nerve	*para vibhuti*	superior *vibhuti*
pareccha	by another's will	*parinama vada*	the theory of Brahman changing into the world
paroksha	hearsay or indirect	*Pasyanti*	a stage in uttering sound
phala	fruit; the result of an act	*phala chaitanyam*	knowledge
phala data	dispenser of the results of our acts	*phala sruti*	description of the result of an act
Pisachas	demons	*poorna*	full
pradakshina	going round a sacred person or place	*pradeepta*	Shining brightly
prajna	the individual being in sleep	*prajnana*	full consciousness
prajnana ghana	full consciousness	*prakriti*	nature, *Maya*
pralaya	dissolution (of the world)	*Pramana*	means of valid knowledge
pramata (*r*)	knower; cogniser	*pramoda*	joy which is higher than *moda*

prana	vital air; life-force; breath; the air which goes up	*pranamaya kosa*	sheath of *prana* or the vital air
pranasakti	the power of the vital forces	*pranava*	another term for OM
pranayama	regulation of breathing	*prapatti*	surrender
prapti	attainment	*prarabdha*	that part of one's karma which is to be worked out in this life
prasad (a)	grace: food etc., which has been offered to Brahman and afterwards distributed among the devotees	*prasthana trayi*	the most important three body of scriptures, The Bhagavad Gita, the Brahma Sutras & the Upanishads
pratibhasika satya	illusory reality as it appears to a particular individual	*pratikam*	symbol
pratikriya	remedy	*pratyabhijna*	recognition
pratyahara	one of the steps in Raja Yoga; withdrawal	*pratyaksha*	direct; immediate
pravritti marga	path of action	*prayaschitta*	a rite for expiating sin
prayatna	effort	*prema*	love
prithvi (prthvi)	earth	*priya*	joy; dear
puja	ceremonial worship with flowers, water etc.	*punya*	merit
puraka	inhalation	*purana*	old; an ancient book of stories embodying religious symbolism
puri	city	*puriashtaka*	subtle body consisting of eight phases
purna	full	*purusha*	man; applied sometimes to Brahman

purushakara	personal effort	*purva paksha*	arguments advanced by the opponent
purva samskara	latent tendency		
R			
Raja Yoga	the principal system of Yoga as taught by Patanjali	*rajas*	one of the three primal qualities, described as red, the principle of activity
rajju-sarpa	rope-snake; a rope looking like a snake in a dim light	*rasa*	bliss
rasasvada	taste of bliss in the absence of thoughts	*ravi marga*	path of the sun
rechaka	exhalation	*rishi (rshi)*	a seer; a sage
S			
sabdanuviddha	associated with sound	*sad guru*	true guru
sadhak (a)	a spiritual aspirant: one who follows a method of spiritual discipline	*sadhana*	method of spiritual practice
sadhana-chatushtaya	the four qualifications expected in an aspirant	*sadhu*	ascetic; sage
sadhu seva	service rendered to sages	*sadyomukti*	immediate Liberation
saguna	with attributes	*saguna upasana*	meditation on Brahman with attributes
sahaja	natural; one's natural state	*sahaja samadhi*	*samadhi* which comes naturally and is present always
sahasrara	the highest yogic center located in the brain	*sajatiya*	of the same kind
sakshatkaram	direct realisation	*sakshi*	witness; the Self
sakti	power	*sakti pata*	descent of divine power on a person

sama	equal; common	*samanya*	common; general; ordinary
samashti	whole	*samatva*	equality
samjnana	awareness; perception	*samrajya*	empire
samsara	the cycle of births and deaths	*samskara*	innate tendency
samvit	consciousness; knowledge	*samyamana*	one-pointedness of mind
sanchita	(*sanchita* accumulated karma of former births *karma*)	*sandeha*	doubt
sanga	association	*sankalpa*	intention, thought; the ostensible motive of doing a ritual uttered before it is begun
sannidhi	presence	*sannyasi*	an ascetic, one who belongs to the fourth stage of life
santi	peace	*sarira*	body
sariri	dweller in the body	*sarira traya*	the three bodies namely the physical, subtle, and causal
Sarva	all	*sarvajna*	omniscient
sarvajnatvam omniscience		*sastra*	scripture; science
sat	good; existence	*satya*	true; the real
satyam	truth; reality	*sat-chit-ananda*	being consciousness-bliss
sat sanga	association with the wise	*satva*	purity: one of the three primal qualities described as white, the principle of purity and goodness
satvapatti	realisation; one of the seven stages of enlightenment	*sattvik*	pure; relating to *satva,* one of the three constituents of *prakriti*

savikalpa samadhi	A state of concentration in which the distinction between the knowers. knowledge and known is not yet lost	*shadadhara*	the six yogic centers
siddha	one who has acquired supernatural powers and is capable of working miracles; also, a state of accomplishment	*siddhi*	supernatural powers; realisation; attainment
sishya	disciple	*sraddha*	faith
Sivoham	I am Siva.	*sloka*	a stanza in Sanskrit
smriti	Memory: scriptures based on the Vedas.	*soham*	I am He (Brahman)
sravana	hearing of the truth from the guru	*Sparsha*	touch
sphurana	manifestation	*srota*	hearer
srishti drishti	gradual creation	*srotra*	ear
sruti	scripture	*sthitaprajna*	one who is established in wisdom
sthula	physical	*sthula sarira*	physical body
sthiti	being	*stotram*	a hymn of praise
subhechcha	desire for enlightenment; one of the seven stages of enlightenment	*suddha*	pure
sukha	happiness	*sukha asana*	easy and comfortable posture of sitting
sukshma	subtle	*sukshma sarira*	the subtle body
sunya	blank; void	*sushumna*	the name of a yogic nerve

sushupti	dreamless sleep	*sutra*	string; aphorism
suvasana	good tendency	*svagata*	within itself
svapna	dream	*svarga*	heaven
svaroopa (*swarupa*)	nature; real form	*swaraj*	independence
swatantra	independence	*swechcha*	of one's own will
T			
taijas	the individual being in dream	*tamas*	darkness; ignorance; one of the three primal qualities described as black; the principle of inertia
tanha	thirst (for living)	*tan matras*	elements in their subtle forms
tanmaya	full of the Self	*tanumanasa*	tenuous mind; one of the seven stages of enlightenment
tapas (*tapasya*)	austerity	*tapobhrashta*	one who has fallen away from his austerities
tapta-aya-pindavat	like a red-hot iron ball	*tattva*	truth, essence of a thing
tejas	effulgence	*tejomaya*	full of light
tejo rupa	of the form of light	*tirtha*	a sacred river or tank
triputi	triad like seer, seen and seeing	*turavu* (Tamil)	renunciation
turya (*turiya*)	the fourth state beyond waking, dreaming, and sleeping	*turyaga*	beyond words; one of the seven stages of enlightenment
tyaga	giving up		
U			
udasinam	indifference	*upadesa*	spiritual instruction
upadhi	limiting adjunct	*upasaka*	one who meditates
upasana	meditation	*upasana sthana*	seat of meditation

V			
vachyartha	literal meaning	*vada*	theory; disputation
vaikhari	one of the stages in the formation of sound; audible sound	*Vaikuntha*	the abode of Vishnu
vairagya	dispassion; non-attachment	*Vaishnavite*	a worshipper of Vishnu
varnasrama dharma	*dharma* of the various castes and stages of life	*vasana*	habit of the mind; latent tendency or impression
vasana kshaya	cessation of *Vasana's*	*vastutah*	in reality
vayu	air	*vibhakti* separation	
vibhuti	sacred ashes; Brahman's glory; supernatural power	*vichara*	enquiry
vichara marga	the spiritual path of enquiry	*vicharana*	investigation; one of the seven stages of enlightenment
videha mukta	One who is liberated after death.	*videha mukti*	liberation after death
vidya	knowledge; learning	*vijatiya*	of a different kind
vijnana	special knowledge; spiritual knowledge	*vijnanamaya kosa*	sheath of intellect
vijnanatman	the ignorant Self	*vijnata*	knower
vikshepa	diversity	*vikshipta*	Distracted.
viparita	*contrary*	*Virat*	totality of gross beings
visesha	particular; special	*vishaya*	object
visishta	qualified	*visishtadvaitin*	one who believes in a modified form of non- duality
visranti	repose	*Visva*	the individual being in the waking state

visvarupa	(*darsana*) Brahman seen as the universe.	*visvarupa darsana*	Brahman seen as the universe.
vivechana	discrimination	*viyoga*	separation
vritti	modification of the mind	*vyaptam*	pervaded
vyashti	part	*vyavahara*	(*vyavaharika*) empirical
vyavahara satya	phenomenal existence		
Y			
yaga	ritualistic sacrifice	*yajna*	sacrifice
yoga	union (with the Supreme Being)	*yogabhrashta*	one who has slipped from the yoga
yogarudha	one who has attained yoga	*Yogiraja*	king of yogis
yugapat srishti	simultaneous creation		

Vasudeva Kutumbakam – The world is one family

Om Shanti Shanti Shanti.

On Sale:

Tvam – 21ˢᵗ Century Bhagavad Gita Volume 1 - Chapters 1 to 6

Amazon link:

https://www.amazon.in/TVAM-21st-Century-Bhagavad-Summary/dp/B0CZ9FML53

Notion Press link:

https://notionpress.com/read/tvam

<u>**Upcoming Books:**</u>

Bhagavad Gita Volume 3 - Chapters 13 to 18

Asi will be an introduction to our relationship with the Divine.

Asi – Merging the individual SELF to the Supreme Self.

The final 6 Chapters are on the unique special and spiritual relationship between the Divine and Man - leading us to the Union of our two selves.

Our exit from this life into the lap of the divine cosmos and our plannings for a new body, new birth. The relationship between Knower, Known, Knowledge and Knowing (Gyana) is finally revealed!

The Five Great Elements (Panch Mahabhuta) are the building blocks of the Universe

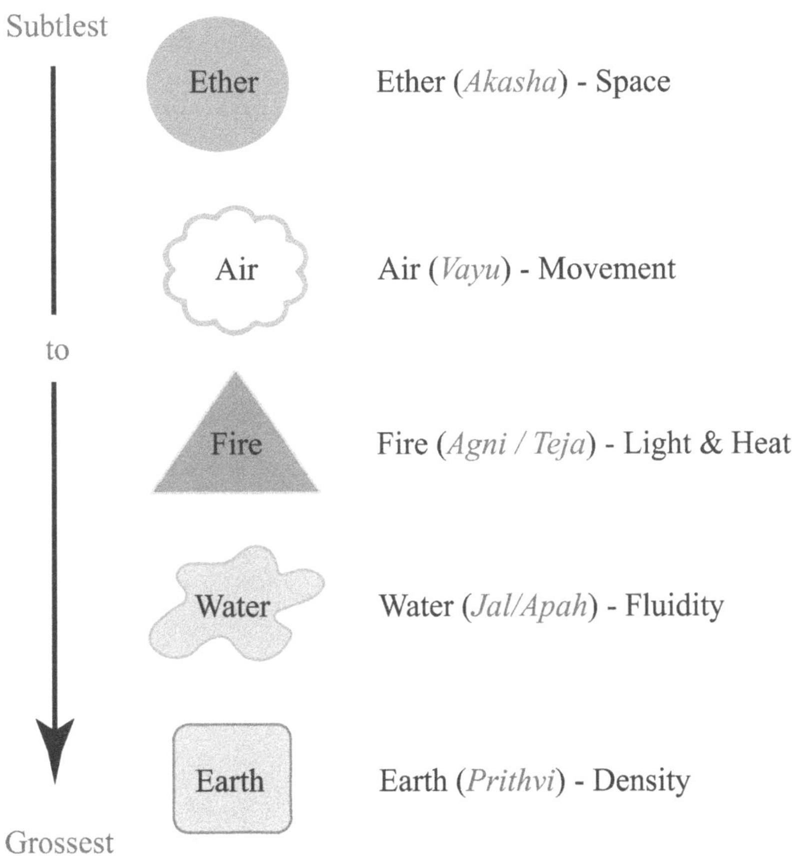

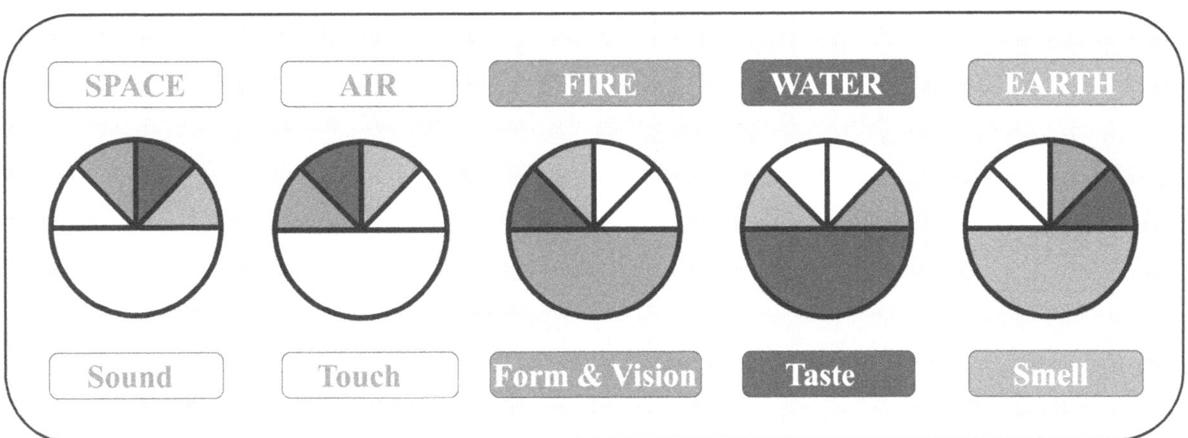

Illustration by Sunita Malhotra

The **three Gunas - Sattva, Rajas & Tamas** pervade the entire Universe.
By their permutations and combinations, infinite number of forms & properties are created.

The 3 Gunas (Triple Qualities) of Cosmic Nature

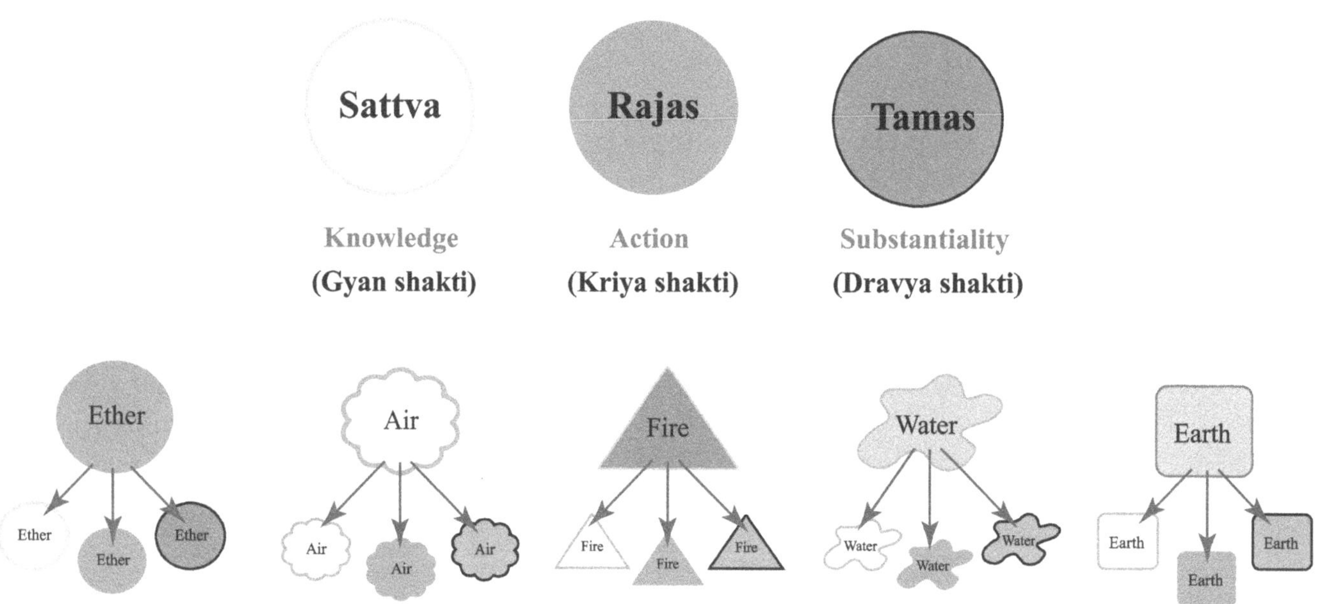

The 3 Gunas pervade & act on the entire creation and also on each of
the 5 Great Elements (Panch Mahabhuta)

Illustration by Sunita Malhotra

The inner instruments are reflected from the total Satvic aspect of the Great Elements
Panch Mahabhuta

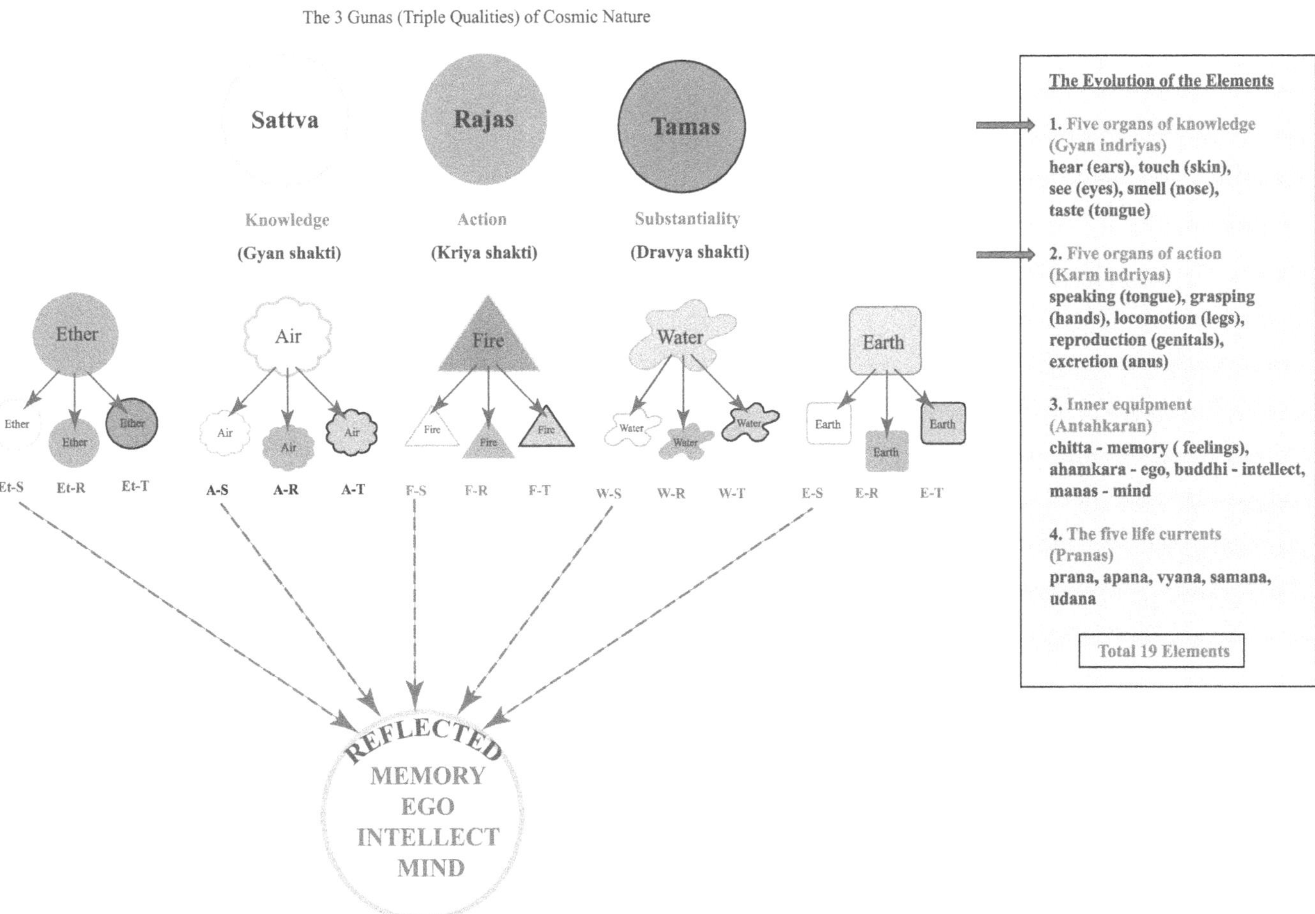

These are the inner instruments

Illustration by Sunita Malhotra

The five organs of knowledge & their abilities / faculties are formed from the Satvic aspect of
each of the 5 Great Elements - Panch Mahabhuta

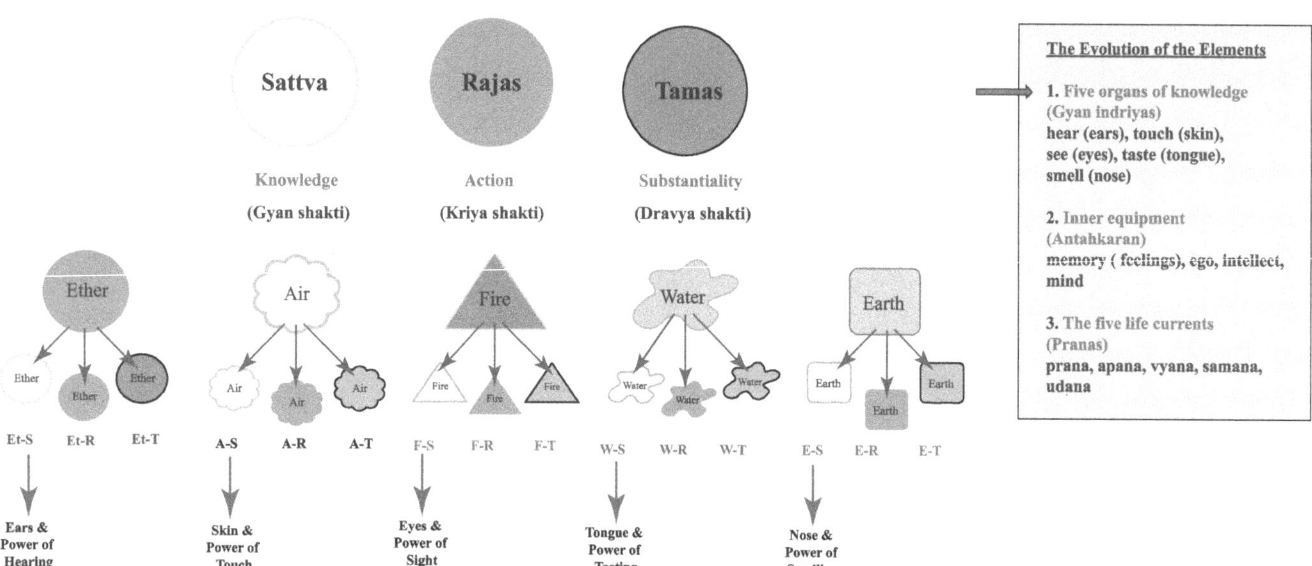

The five organs of action & their abilities / faculties are formed from the Rajasic aspect
of each of the 5 Great Elements - Panch Mahabhuta

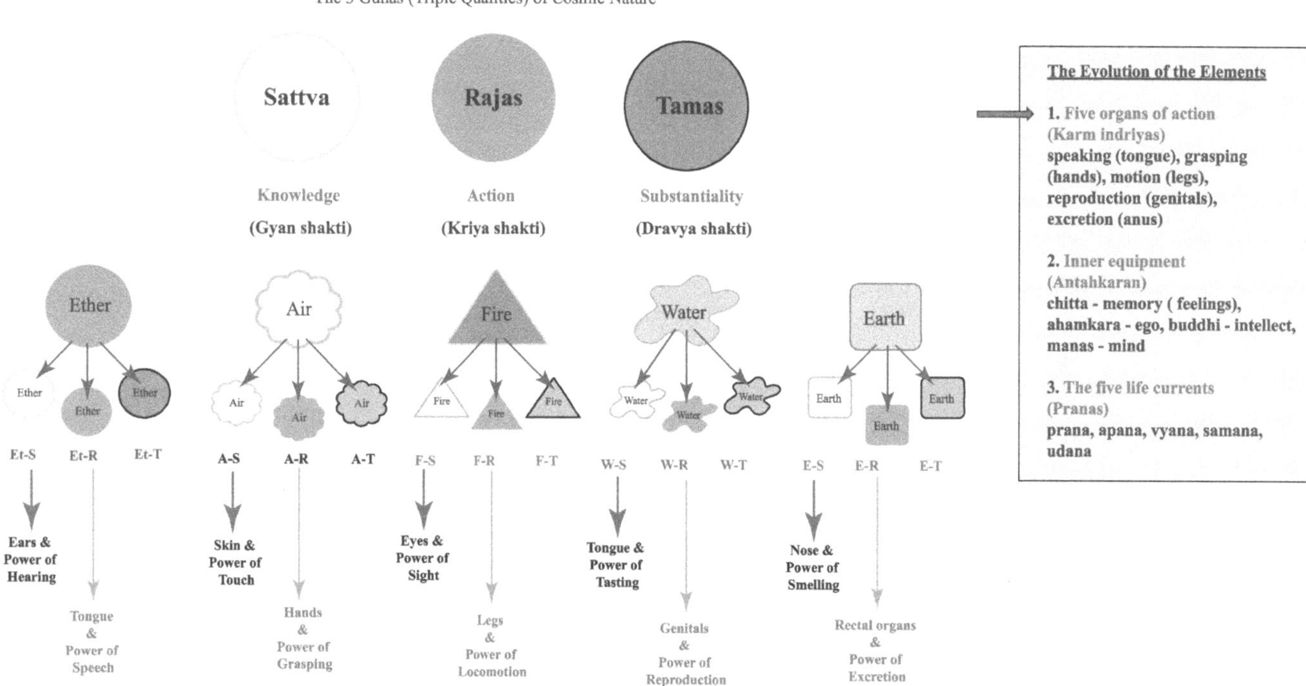

Illustration by Sunita Malhotra

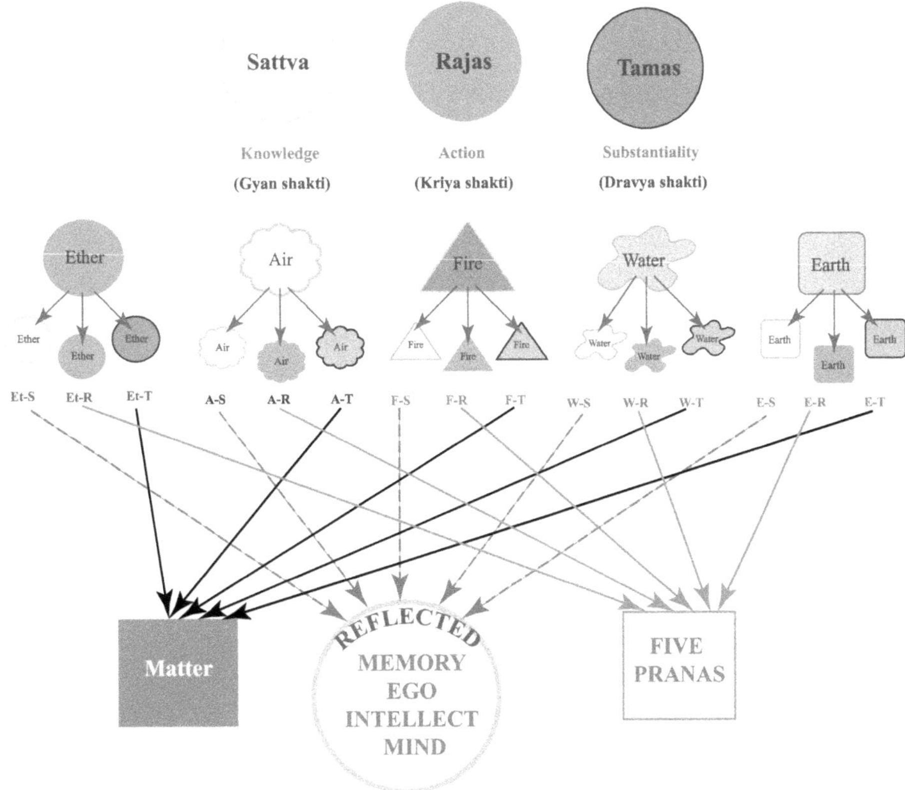

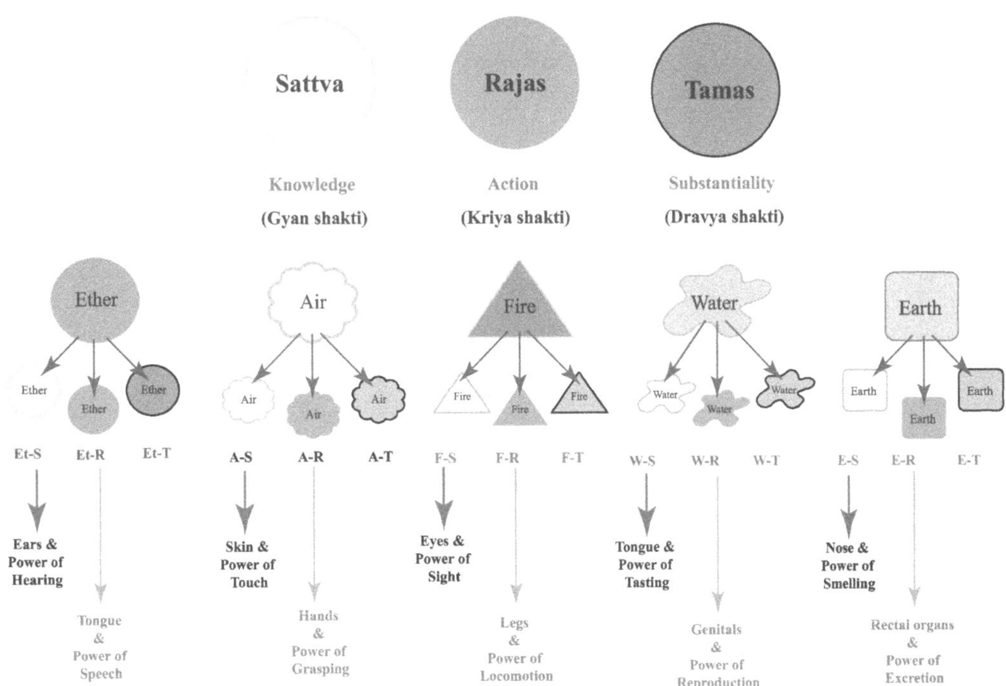

Illustration by Sunita Malhotra

Anuradha Mahajan

My journey into Vēdānta

Initially I took this endeavor for self-discovery which quickly metamorphosed into a labor of love and research.

I am blessed to be able to bring you **Tat - Volume 2 of the Bhagavad Gita** with the hope that it will lead the reader into introspection as it did me in 2009, when I picked it up for the very first time.

My journey into Vēdānta began with a group study of the Bhagavad Gita held in Bahrain. Our friend and guide Ms. Sangeeta Dhown hosted a 4-year endeavor helping a small group us to delve deep into Vēdānta.

In 2013, I began teaching and as a result learning this most revered text and have since continuously conducted year long. After a 12-year deep dive into the Bhagavad Gita, I bring to you the collated summary of this study.

Along with my dear friend and mentor Sajni Vaidya, who assisted in tabulating the knowledge, this edition has been compiled with numerous illustrations, diagrams and interpretations. We apologize if we may have erroneously misinterpreted any content however the intent is purely to bring about a clear understanding and insight into our revered scripture.

I dedicate this work to all my peers who attended the learning sessions over the last 11 years resulting in many discussions, debates and arguments to further achieve clarity of this esoteric Gyan.

My dream is that educational institutions across India and the rest of the world include this study in their classrooms and in their homes so our children at the grassroot are empowered with this enlightening and enlivening knowledge that is secreted in our wisdom-saturated scriptures. Which have not yet found their way into our mainstream school study.

It is time that we bring the 21st Century Bhagavad Gita to the world with clarity and relevance such that it becomes inseparable from our very being.

This knowledge is universal and is what is known as Sanatana Dharma – truly applicable to all of mankind.

To my daughter Riva and husband Rishi, I dedicate this book and wish that we all rediscover our pure spiritual space, our Consciousness.

Anuradha Mahajan
Dubai – United Arab Emirates

Dr. Sajni Vaidya

My journey towards spiritualism started at an early age when I accompanied my mother to various Satsang's and kirtans and spiritual discourses. She read verses daily from both the Bhagavad Gita and the Sukhmani path [from Sikhism]. Though we were not taught religion formally at home, what we imbibed was by observing her faith, that never faltered even in dire situations. Education in an English Medium School meant that we learnt to pray daily to Christ, too. My childhood was spent in a cosmopolitan society where we celebrated all festivals, of all faiths.

The quest to seek, know more and understand the basics of Sanatana Dhrama began after marriage. My In-laws follow the BAPS Swaminarayan Satsang, wherein our family values and our family ties have strengthened. Parul didi (sister), a lady from the Chinmaya Mission was my first Gita teacher in Mumbai. After moving to Bahrain, it took me many years to find Anuradha Mahajan who re-ignited the spark in me to continue my spiritual journey. She introduced me to the "Science of God Realisation" by Parmahansa Yogananda and led me to Ms. Sangeeta Dhown who shed extensive light on Vēdānta in the home study courses she conducts. I continued learning with her for ten years.

What impressed me the most, when studying the Bhagavad Gita by Sri Yogananda, was the scientific evidence and understanding of the functioning of the Macrocosm (Brahman) and the Microcosm (us) – the Creator and his Creation. This book opened a world of amazing knowledge and insight where the pieces of the creation puzzle fell into place along with many unanswered questions of a lifetime.

I gained more insight by listening to Gurudeva Sri Sri Ravi Shankar's commentaries on the various Upanishads, the Bhagavad Gita and the Patanjali Yoga Sutras, and also during my training as a certified Yoga teacher, at the Yoga Institute, Mumbai.

Encouraged by Sangeeta Dhown, I started conducting teaching sessions leading a host of seekers on their individual journey of knowing the Bhagavad Gita. These classes are ongoing as the thirst for this spiritual pursuit is ever existent. I believe sharing knowledge is also the best way to keep learning! It is my mission and my dream to introduce this great guiding knowledge to as many aspirants as possible. The Bhagavad Gita guides us into leading a fulfilling life of spiritual contentment, peace and freedom.

I am honored and grateful for the opportunity to share what I have understood, with the hope that it will ignite in the reader, a quest to know, learn, evolve and research our very own revered scripture…

I wish to dedicate this book to my husband Dr Nanubhai Vaidya and my son Aditya, as we traverse this journey of Self-Discovery together!

Dr. Sajni Vaidya,
Manama, Kingdom of Bahrain

Amazon India link:

https://amzn.in/d/5YKcxT1

Notion Press:

https://notionpress.com/read/tvam?utm_source=share_publish_email&utm_medium=whatsapp

Acknowledgement

To **Sangeeta Dhown** for sharing the detailed Creation chart. As always, she remains aligned in her quest to create greater understanding and clarity for Vedanta studies.

To **Sunita Malhotra** for generously sharing her meticulous and detailed illustrations on the building blocks of Creation and their elements, resulting in adding and enhancing further our comprehension of **TAT.**

In gratitude, Thank you Sangeeta & Sunita

Acknowledgement

We are grateful to Ajesh Ambili for contributing his valuable technical skills to this body of work. An experienced Graphic designer & Illustrator, Ajesh helped us in reformatting the text, the tables and the illustrations, in line with our specifications. With patience, dedication and cooperation, he helped complete several hundred edits and re edits during the past year. We wish him all the success tempered with spirituality in his unique onward journey.

Ajesh Ambili Graphic Designer & Illustrator Extraordinaire
Thiruvananthapuram - Dubai